My Life NOW

Essays by a
Child Sex Trafficking Survivor

MARY KNIGHT

My Life
NOW

Contents

Prologue

Maria Socolof, 8/20/22

Our stories may differ, but traumatization can occur from many varied underlying events. I had the pleasure of meeting Mary Knight in 2021 through the advocacy group Incest AWARE. After I enjoyed a successful twenty-two-year career as an environmental health scientist, my life's focus shifted when I was forced to face a past trauma that resulted in debilitating chronic pain. Unable to continue my hard-earned career, I had to concentrate on healing and ultimately found myself compelled to tell my story. I had recently published my memoir and was ready and determined to continue speaking out on behalf of others who have suffered as a result of childhood sexual trauma.

During Incest AWARE's inaugural meeting, survivor advocates shared about their past work and what they hoped to accomplish in the future. It was then that I learned of Mary's film projects. I was immediately intrigued, and later impressed when I had the privilege of viewing them.

As I continued to get to know Mary through her impressive website and later from direct one-on-one conversations, I learned that our backstories are vastly different. Yet we formed a strong connection based on our shared healing experiences, and I knew I wanted to support her valuable efforts. I have read Mary's essays that follow, and I predict they will capture your hearts and souls and inspire healing. Kindly indulge me while I set the stage for them.

Trauma is how an individual reacts to an unbearable situation. It affects each of us in our own unique way. The US's Substance Abuse and Mental Health Services Administration describes it in this way:

> *"Individual trauma results from an event, series of events, or set of circumstances that is experienced by an individual as physically or emotionally harmful or life threatening and that has lasting adverse effects on the individual's functioning and physical, social, emotional, or spiritual well-being."*

In many ways contrasting Mary's upbringing, I grew up in what would be considered a safe and loving environment under the guidance of my two devoted parents in our happy suburban home. Yet I was sexually violated on one occasion by my sibling, who had been sexually abused outside of the family. Not fully understanding the consequences of his actions, he passed his trauma on to me. The unfathomable assault on my body by my beloved and trusted sibling caused my protective brain to put this memory in the far recesses of my subconscious, where it stayed for thirty-two years.

Repressing a memory, clinically called *dissociative amnesia*, is rather common among trauma and sexual abuse survivors. In fact, research indicates that 32 percent of trauma survivors[1] and 42 percent of sexual abuse survivors[2] do not remember their trauma or abuse for a period of time, lasting anywhere from days to decades.

This is a natural coping method we use to mentally escape from the horror of a situation and is well recognized in neuroscience and trauma research. There are many conditions that might increase the likelihood that a survivor will not remember their abuse. These include the younger the victim; increased frequency, duration, or severity of the abuse; increased number of perpetrators; psychological closeness, such as that with a relative; lack of support, particularly from one's mother when disclosing the abuse; and a natural tendency for some people to dissociate.[3] This is not to say that seemingly minor events won't cause dissociative amnesia or have long-lasting effects. What causes us to not remember can vary significantly.

Not until I was forty-two years old did I recall that my brother molested me when I was ten. I later learned that repressing the memory was a survival strategy. It allowed me to remove from my memory what I couldn't fully process at the time. It allowed me to function in spite of an incomprehensible act. It allowed me to live under the same roof as someone who had violated my body—and my trust. It allowed me to keep my family together and to stay with my parents, who didn't come to my rescue (to no fault of their own), but whom I depended on for survival.

1—Diana M. Elliott, "Traumatic Events: Prevalence and Delayed Recall in the General Population." *Journal of Consulting and Clinical Psychology* 65, no. 5 (1997): 811 in Wolf and Nochajski, 2013.[3]

2—Diana M. Elliott and John Briere, "Posttraumatic Stress Associated with Delayed Recall of Sexual Abuse: A General Population Study." *Journal of Traumatic Stress* 8, no. 4 (1995): 629–647.

3—Molly R. Wolf and Thomas H. Nochajski, "Child Sexual Abuse Survivors with Dissociative Amnesia: What's the Difference?" *Journal of Child Sexual Abuse* 22, no. 4 (2013): 462–480.

I had made a cryptic attempt to tell my parents at the time, as evidenced by a note that my parents found in their attic thirty-three years after the fact. Without explaining what had happened, I asked my mother if I could sleep with her. This was not a common request from ten-year-old me, and since my mother didn't know what had occurred, she rejected my subtle cry for help.

My young mind learned that my parents didn't protect me. This, however, was in stark contrast to my consciously lived childhood of love and support from wonderful parents.

While my charmed life went on, my subconscious held a dark secret. The one-time violation and my mother's rejection (as I perceived it at the time) seem to have been enough for me to be traumatized and to push the memory far away for decades.

My mind-blowing recollection was ultimately corroborated by the perpetrator himself. When I asked him point-blank about it, he immediately took full responsibility for what he did to me. I was immensely grateful for this acknowledgement, and yet I spent the next dozen-plus years working through my trauma via various bodywork and psychological therapies, as well as many self-care approaches. I dug into my mind and body to find deeply buried emotions that were holding me hostage and causing me chronic physical pain. Fear, anger, confusion, shame, unworthiness. Through all this work and countless hours of cathartic writing, I'm now able to tell my story. In doing so, I have learned that I am not alone in my suffering and that millions of others are living with the aftereffects of trauma too.

Mary reminded me not to compare my abuse to hers and not to minimize what happened to me. Even if what I experienced seemed insignificant compared to the abuse she and others have suffered, I was still traumatized by something that my child-brain could not process, and I need to respect and honor that fact. That is how we heal.

As you embark on reading Mary's account of her upbringing, you will encounter a far different history. You will understand that it is only logical that her brain also did the best it could to protect her by forgetting. When considering her story, it's difficult for most of us to imagine how truly cruel some people can be, especially to their own children. It's almost as hard to believe that someone who was surrounded by so much evil could grow into such a kind and loving person. But that's exactly what Mary has done. She shares snippets of her life through a series of essays and a short story, which together show examples of her resilience in the face of horrific abuse.

Through the powerfully honest telling of her personal experiences, she provides tips and advice for those of us who are on our own healing journeys and exposes difficult truths to the world at large in an effort to promote prevention and affect change. Mary's inspiring narratives of how evil does not have to reign are a testament to how the human heart, mind, and soul can exhibit the strength to overcome such adversity.

I ask you, the readers, to take care of yourselves by heeding the book's trigger warnings, but be reassured that inspiring and hopeful messages are contained within. Know that you'll come out at the end in awe of a woman who had seemingly insurmountable odds against her. She has triumphed over deep, dark emotional and physical pain and now lives in a world of light and love, bringing positivity and hope to those around her.

Although Mary and I had quite different childhood experiences, we share many commonalities. We were both traumatized by family members, we both repressed our memories for years, we both have lived with debilitating chronic pain, we both have undergone many types of therapies and tried numerous self-care approaches to further our healing, we both created websites detailing how we have healed, we both have penned our stories, and we both are driven toward advocacy work. As such, we are building awareness of the diversity of childhood sexual trauma, providing support to other survivors, and demonstrating that there is a path to healing.

Besides Mary's film documentaries, she continues to speak out in podcasts and other media outlets. Mary and I have also recently collaborated with the TWC Clubhouse—a safe online place to meet others who have experienced trauma—to provide classes based on our healing experiences. With the completion of her captivating memoir, know that as an advocate, Mary will not stop here. She continues her passionate drive to help fellow survivors and to work with other advocates to provide support and comfort to those needing it and to make the world a safer place.

Let Mary's story allow you to reflect on how traumas can affect us and how healing is possible—whatever the underlying experiences.

—Maria Socolof

Author of *The Invisible Key: Unlocking the Mystery of My Chronic Pain*

MS in environmental health sciences, Harvard School of Public Health

Founding member of the nonprofit 5WAVES, Inc: Worldwide Awareness, Voice, Education, and Support for Those Affected by Sibling Sexual Trauma

www.healingfromchronicpain.com

Introduction

Exercise Self-Care While Reading

My memoir is a collection of essays. Each contains an element of hope. These essays can be read in any order. My memories of childhood abuse are so bizarre that I decided to spare myself and my readers the trauma of adhering to chronological order.

Every essay has an individualized trigger warning—categorized as low, medium, high, or extremely high. The most common trigger warning is low, meaning that the material is not likely to be disturbing or upsetting. The second most common trigger warning is medium, meaning it contains at least one specific example of severe child abuse.

I have not met anyone who is unaffected by the three essays that I have labeled with an "extremely high" trigger warning. I am often asked to elaborate on the extraordinarily cruel assaults I endured as a child. I would not have included these essays if I thought curiosity was the only motivation people had for wanting graphic descriptions. I find that some people study my life to learn how to better protect children. Professional psychotherapists have assured me that my detailed accounts benefit them in their work with survivors of extreme child abuse. If you are on the fence about whether to read an essay or not, my advice is to choose self-care. If you want to read an essay because you are wondering whether you and I have commonalities in our abuse histories, please ask a trusted friend or counselor to preview the essay before you read it yourself.

I cannot overemphasize that it is okay to refrain from reading the most triggering essays. For many years, I was in a writing group with mature women. We each had ten minutes to read aloud something that we had written during the week. My turn came, and I watched silently as over half of the group members stood up and filed out the door. To be fair, I always prefaced my reading by saying, "I write about the horrors I experienced as a child. It will not hurt my feelings if you feel a need to leave the room. I would rather you leave during my turn than to be triggered by my content in any way that is unhealthy for you."

Synopses of Essays Included in This Memoir

The following synopses and the full essays in this memoir contain many terms associated with child abuse and related issues. Readers may not be familiar with some of them. A glossary of selected terms is included at the end of this introduction.

"Becoming Mrs. Brown" | Trigger Warning: Medium

When I was a very young child, my elderly neighbor Mrs. Brown cooked salty oatmeal for me on her ancient wood-burning stove. I thought she looked elegant wearing her pearl necklace with her shabby housedress. She was unable to rescue me from my violent childhood, and yet, she saved my life by loving me. I gave this essay a medium trigger warning only because it contains one disturbing detail.

"Psychological Benefits of Delayed Recall and Recovered Memories" | Trigger Warning: Low

I recovered my memories of childhood abuse when I was an adult. Many people want a simple explanation for delayed recall and recovered memories. I do not have one. It is hard to understand how someone can forget horrendous abuse. I am sure that my life is better because my mind allowed me to place memories of abuse into a compartment that I could not open until age thirty-seven, when I felt safe enough to do so. This essay describes the advantages of my delayed recall of the many traumatic events during my childhood.

"How I Know My Recovered Memories of Incest Are True" | Trigger Warning: Low

Consisting of a ten-item list, this piece is a must-read for anyone whose inner critic discounts the memories that they know within their deepest self to be true.

"Family" | Trigger Warning: Medium

This essay describes my family background. It contains information about my biological relatives that I have never before shared publicly. I also include individuals not related by blood or marriage who have become part of my family.

"My Parents were KKK members and Pedophiles" | Trigger Warning: Extremely High

When I was eight years old, I witnessed a Ku Klux Klan atrocity. This essay recounts the story. A reader described this account as "beautifully written, and the most brutal thing I have ever read."

"My Relationship with Religion" | Trigger Warning: Medium

This piece is based on the first and only sermon that I ever have delivered. It describes the complicated connection that I have with faith communities. I was raised in a denomination that did not allow women in the pulpit. As a little girl, sitting perfectly erect on an uncomfortable wooden pew, I would ponder how the preacher could word his homily better. This sermon has a medium trigger warning because it contains a few details of my childhood abuse by church leaders.

"Child Sexual Abuse in Church Settings: My Experiences and Recommendations for Prevention" | Trigger Warning: Medium

For all my essays except this one, I anticipate that a large proportion of the audience will be survivors, survivor advocates, and professionals who work with survivors. This essay may be the exception. My hope is that it will be read by as many church decision-makers as possible. If you are a church member, please ask the leaders of your church to read this essay. Young children deserve policies that are stronger than the usual Safe Sanctuary protocols.

"Familial Sex Trafficking and Ritualistic Abuse" | Trigger Warning: Medium

I gave this essay only a medium trigger warning because, although its content gives a complete description of the subject matter, I left out detailed examples.

"Examples of Ritualistic Abuse" and "Examples of Familial Sex Trafficking" | Trigger Warnings: Extremely High

These two essays give horrendous examples and could not be any more triggering than they are. I strongly suggest that you do not read both in the same sitting.

"The Magic of Creativity" | Trigger Warning: Medium

This essay follows my journey to become a writer and film-maker, starting with a creativity class that I took at age forty. It gives behind-the-scenes information about each of my films, as well as about my writings.

"My Encounters with the False Memory Syndrome Foundation" | Trigger Warning: Low

This essay describes the conversations and confrontations that I have had with proponents of the False Memory Syndrome Foundation (FMSF), which was established for the purpose of discounting recovered memories of child abuse. It has a low trigger warning because it does not include details of child abuse. However, the essay may be maddening to some survivors because of the long-running controversy about the veracity of recovered memories. I include background details about the interviews that I conducted with FMSF proponents for my personal documentary *Am I Crazy? My Journey to Determine if My Memories Are True.*

"True Memories" | Trigger Warning: Low

This is the only essay in this book not written by me. It was written by chronic-pain-recovery therapist and coach Anna Holtzman. Like me, she recalled her childhood sexual trauma when she was in her thirties. I hope my readers will be as impressed as I am with her simple, easily understood language and logic about her remembering process.

"How I Healed from Trauma-Induced Chronic Pain" | Trigger Warning: Low

The question I am asked the most often is "how did you heal?" The inquiry seems simple, but the answer is complicated. In the end, each person needs to find their own path to recovery. I explain mine in detail in this 10,000-word essay. My approaches to healing are grouped into nine categories. The essay includes practical suggestions and specific resources. Helping others heal is my passion.

"My Life Now" | Trigger Warning: Low

This essay describes my current life, which is filled with joy, love, and children.

"Ruby's Heaven" | Trigger Warning: Low

This short story is included amid my personal essays. It is the only fictional piece in this book. It is an uplifting story about my angel connection with my mother. "Ruby's Heaven" is truly heartwarming. I put it at the end because it can be a nice bedtime story for grown-ups!

Timeline of Major Life Events

My earliest memory is of being sexually abused. I cannot give an exact age when the abuse started, but it was before I had words. I was unbelievably young the first time that I was touched in ways that can only be understood by adult minds. This fact makes the abuse especially hard to describe.

I also do not have a clear memory of the last time that I was sexually abused. I was a victim of incest and sex trafficking throughout my teenaged years.

- **1955:** Born in Seattle, Washington
- **1971:** Moved to Denver, Colorado
- **1973:** Graduated from high school
- **1973–1974:** Attended York College (a conservative

Christian College) in York, Nebraska; received an associate's degree

- **1974–1976:** Attended Harding College (a conservative Christian college) in Searcy, Arkansas; received a Bachelor of Arts degree in psychology

- **1976–1978:** Employed at Colorado Christian Services (Denver, Colorado) as an adoption worker

- **1978–1980:** Attended graduate school at University of Texas at Arlington; received Master of Social Work degree

- **1980:** Married my first husband

- **1980–1985:** Employed at the Children's Home of Lubbock in Lubbock, Texas, as the adoption supervisor

- **1984:** My older son born

- **1985:** Moved to Denver, Colorado, for my first husband's job

- **1984–1988:** Employed as a part-time social worker

- **1986:** My younger son born

- **1988:** Moved to Dallas, Texas, for my first husband's job

- **1988–1991:** Stayed at home full time with my sons

- **1991–2001:** Employed part time as a licensed social worker, completing parenting time evaluations by court orders in contested divorce custody cases and conducting play therapy sessions with children

- **1993:** Began to recover memories of child abuse

- **1995:** Took a creativity class, started writing

- **2001:** Moved back to the Pacific Northwest, to a suburb of Portland, Oregon

- **2001–2007:** Experienced social work burnout. Held various jobs, including real-estate agent and other outside sales positions

- **2003:** Divorced my first husband

- **2006:** Took my first filmmaking class

- **2007:** Renewed my social work license; completed parenting time evaluations by court orders in contested divorce custody cases

- **2010:** Married the love of my life, Jerry Witler

- **2011:** Retired from social work; became full-time filmmaker

- **2013:** Premiered my short film *One Man's Anger, One Woman's Love*

- **2014:** Premiered *Sister Mary's Angel*, PG-13

- **2017:** Premiered *Am I Crazy? My Journey to Determine if My Memories Are True* (55-minute version)

- **2018:** My husband Jerry retired; we moved to Bellingham, Washington

- **2019:** Jerry and I became foster parents

- **2022:** Renewed my social work license to do play therapy with children

- **2022:** Premiered *Am I Crazy? My Journey to Determine if My Memories Are True* (103-minute version)

- **2022:** Premiered *Mothers and Molestation: A Film about Child Abuse*

- **2022:** Published this memoir

Glossary of Selected Terms Used in This Memoir

Delayed Recall: The ability to recollect information acquired earlier (definition from the *American Psychological Association Dictionary of Psychology*). In the context of this memoir, it refers to recollections of childhood abuse after a long period of not having such memories.

Familial Sex Trafficking: A form of sex trafficking in which the child victim is controlled by relatives who allow them to be sexually exploited in exchange for something of value.

Recovered Memory: A memory of a traumatic event, such as sexual abuse, that is experienced typically during childhood and is forgotten and then recalled many years later.

Ritualistic Abuse: Physical and/or sexual child abuse and torture involving either multiple child victims or multiple adult perpetrators or both. Ritualistic abuse often includes the desecration of a sacred symbol. It can include ritualistic murders.

Sex Trafficking: The recruitment, harboring, transportation, provision, obtaining, patronizing, or soliciting of a person for the purpose of a commercial sex act, in which the commercial sex act is induced by force, fraud, or coercion, or in which the person induced to perform such act has not attained eighteen years of age (definition based on federal law).

Survivor: In the context of this memoir, a survivor of child abuse.

Traumatic Event: A shocking, scary, or dangerous experience that can affect someone emotionally and physically. Experiences like natural disasters, acts of violence, as well as car crashes and other accidents all can be traumatic. A trauma event often can impact long-term physical and mental health.

Trigger: A sensory reminder that causes painful memories or certain symptoms to resurface.

Becoming Mrs. Brown

Trigger Warning: Low

·······································

This was a contest speech for Toastmasters International, a worldwide educational organization that teaches public speaking skills. This speech won at the local club level in January 2020.

·······································

Can you remember a time in your childhood when you felt treasured?

To the little blond-haired girl I used to be, Mrs. Brown was grandma, fairy godmother, and Santa Claus all rolled up in one. When she hugged me, I felt cherished. To me, Mrs. Brown was beautiful and elegant. She always wore her pearl necklace, even with a shabby house dress. Before I was old enough to go to kindergarten, I walked to her house on weekday mornings. We lived in the country. I walked a quarter of a mile, but no matter how tired I was, when I saw her house, I would start running.

Mrs. Brown was always excited to see me! When she opened her door and saw me, her eyes lit up. She would say,

"I think the mush is almost ready." I would sit at her round oak table and watch her scoop up the oatmeal she called mush. It was salty. I still love the taste of salty oatmeal. And the aroma of her homemade bread! Her whole little house smelled like home. On my first day of kindergarten, I insisted that Mrs. Brown come with me.

When I was in first grade, my family moved to a new house. I did not see Mrs. Brown anymore. And yet, she saved my life so that, as an adult, I could rescue myself.

I was raised in an upper-middle-class family that looked perfect on the outside, but my earliest memories are of sexual abuse by my parents. Fellow Toastmasters, I know some of you can relate to that kind of childhood. According to research conducted by the Centers for Disease Control and Prevention, one in four women and one in six men have been sexually abused as children. My abuse went even further. My parents prostituted me. I was sex trafficked. A lot of people think human trafficking is something that happens only in other countries, but that is not true. It happened to me, here, in Washington State. I can remember a time when my mother held out her hand to take money from the men.

I know you are wondering why my parents were so cruel to me. I grappled with that question while my parents were alive, while sitting on my parents' graves, in my bed late at night when I could not sleep, and in numerous counseling sessions. I do not have a definitive answer, especially not a succinct one. Good people have trouble comprehending evil.

You may also wonder why I did not tell anyone about my abuse. The reason is that, even during my childhood, I was not cognizant of the abuse except for while it was happening. If it had not been for the gift of delayed recall, the brain's ability to store memories away from the conscience state of mind until a later time, I would not have eaten the food my parents gave me. I could not have gone to school and earned good grades.

I was thirty-seven years old when I remembered. The memories were brutal, but I was comforted by the vivid recollection of what I had always remembered: Mrs. Brown's house, the taste of salty oatmeal, the smell of homemade bread, and the hugs. Oh, those hugs!

I still get counseling as needed, and I take antidepressants, but I have a wonderful life now. I have a great marriage, although my husband sometimes wonders about my many excuses to buy round oak tables. We have not one, not two, but three of them.

Would I have recovered from this abuse had it not been for Mrs. Brown? No!

Was there a moment in your childhood when you felt completely cherished? If so, I want you to let yourself experience that feeling right now. Let it sink in. Close your eyes if you like.

As an adult, I often recognize how much fun Mrs. Brown must have had. I bake homemade bread for our foster children. As I take it out of the oven, the six-year-old, who we refer to as the Energizer Bunny, does his celebration dance.

Are you spending your professional life, or your volunteer time, cherishing children? If so, thank you. Thank you! You may never know the depth of your impact.

To the rest of you, please consider becoming a Mrs. Brown. There are lots of ways to do this. Apply to Big Brothers Big Sisters, volunteer at a school, or simply be kind to children you see in the checkout line at the grocery store.

Even if you cannot rescue a child, you can save that child's life!

Psychological Benefits of Delayed Recall

Trigger Warning: Low

I am certain that my memories of childhood sexual abuse are true.

I did not remember my abuse until I was thirty-seven years old. Even as a child, I had no conscious memory of the atrocities except while they were occurring.

When discussing recovered memories like mine, the focus tends to be on their credibility. Since I no longer need to spend my time and energy determining the validity of my recollections, my attention has turned to examining the many ways that delayed recall benefitted me.

Vacations help us maintain our emotional well-being, especially for those of us with extremely demanding jobs. There is no job as demanding as surviving an abusive childhood. Delayed recall for a child is like taking a vacation from the fear, horror, and shame of the abuse. As a little girl who was molested by both parents, delayed recall gave me a psychological vacation from the abuse.

My speech teacher

Delayed recall enabled me to not only do well in school but also find comfort there. I was always aware that my parents were very critical and that they yelled a lot. In contrast, my teachers were kind and respectful. They complimented me when I worked hard. School was a haven for me, a calm place where things made sense.

Friendships have nourished me throughout my life. My social skills were well honed in grade school. In school, I associated with high achievers. Many of my long-term friends have graduate degrees.

I had a master's degree in social work before I recalled my abuse. Two of my articles were published in professional journals. I was appointed by judges to do divorce custody and parenting time evaluations. I testified as a mental health expert on a regular basis. I now realize that the respect that

I received from judges and attorneys was one of the factors that empowered me to trust myself enough to remember what deep down inside I always knew.

I was making strides in becoming self-actualized. I read books on codependency, then took a class about it, and eventually joined a twelve-step group for adult children of alcoholics. (Neither of my parents were alcoholics, but my mother acknowledged alcoholism on the part of her deceased father.) I finally realized that the problems in my first marriage were not all mine, and I insisted on marriage counseling. I began finding ways to have fun, like acting at a community theater. I started dressing in brighter colors, and I quit choosing styles that hid my figure.

During my childhood, forgetting allowed me to develop intellectually and emotionally in tandem with my peers. Remembering what happened to me as a child turned my world upside down. In no way do I want to minimize that fact. Still, I am thankful for my delayed recall.

In college, I studied Maslow's hierarchy of needs. In his five-tier model of human needs, Maslow suggests that you must fulfill the lower needs before it is possible to fulfill the higher ones. The lowest needs are physical, such as food, water, and shelter. The next level is safety and security. After that is belongingness and a sense of community. Then come esteem needs, which are associated with accomplishments. Lastly, according to Maslow, is the need to become self-actualized.

When I first learned about Maslow's hierarchy, it did not make sense to me. I argued with my college professor, insisting that starving people can become self-actualized. I now realize that, on a deeper level, I was speaking for myself. My parents led a double life. In their upper middle-class respectable existence, my physical needs were met.

The life that my mind kept hidden from me included food deprivation and torture.

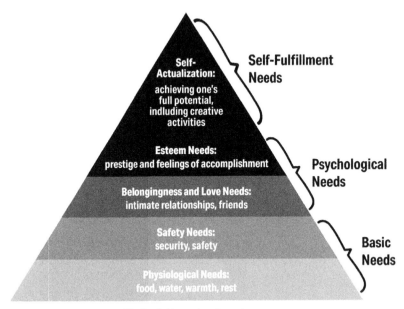

Maslow's hierarchy of needs

For me, Maslow's triangle was upside down. I began to meet my higher needs before having the solid foundation that permitted me to process what happened to me as a child. I had the skills and connections by then to enable me to find a sense of community and family that did not include my abusers. My professional accomplishments gave me the confidence to make it on my own.

My safety needs were the last to be satisfied, partly because I had been drawn to men who, like my father, were untrustworthy. I finally feel safe in my own home. Jerry and I married ten years ago. We live in a house we easily can afford. The view from our deck fills me with joy daily. Creative activities, which are a form of self-actualization, absorb a large portion of my time.

Rather than an upside-down or a right-side-up triangle, my process of remembering has consisted of lines that are far from straight. I still have new memories occasionally. Some are brutal, even in the midst of the good life that I now enjoy. To cope, I take good care of myself. I have a pajama day, indulge in long baths, relax my body with yoga and massage, dance, journal, and hike alone or with my husband. At the same time, I remember myself as the child who did not have these opportunities.

I do not push myself to remember. I am fine with unclear memories. I do not need all the details. The only memories that I need are those that will help me or another person.

While I celebrate everyone's path to recovery, I am glad mine included delayed recall. I do not know how I would have survived my childhood without it, but it did more than save my life. Delayed recall allowed me to have a life worth living.

At 38—one year after recovering memories

How I Know
My Childhood
Memories Are True

Trigger Warning: Low

....

Caution for survivors: Don't judge yourself harshly if you
don't have as much corroboration of your memories as I
do. Most survivors don't. Remember that the most important things in life can never be proven in a court of law.

....

1. **General Health:** I got well! After experiencing
    almost continuous pain from my earliest memories,
    I am now pain free. I thought everyone was like
    me until, at age thirty-two, I asked the other moms
    of toddlers who were in a playgroup with me and
    found out they didn't suffer from pain every day.
    I then went to a doctor and was diagnosed with
    fibromyalgia, which I no longer have.

2. **Specific Physical Symptoms:** Pain related to mem-
    ories subsided after I worked through the memory.
    For example, while I was getting a massage, I

began to regain a memory of a gun being pointed at my head. I had a sharp pain on the left side of my scalp. The pain would subside and then come back whenever I had a scalp massage. After I fully regained the memory and dealt with it emotionally, the pain vanished.

3. **A Lack of Motivation to Falsely Accuse:** Recovering memories of child abuse did not result in my financial gain. In fact, I was disinherited by my father, a multimillionaire. Even so, I am glad I remembered what he did and had confronted him before he died.

4. **Confirmation from Relatives:** I have an aunt and four cousins with memories like mine.

5. **Excellent Psychotherapy:** I knew how to choose good counselors, and I did so. I decided to use hypnosis as a way to regain memories, and I taped the hypnosis sessions. These tapes prove that the psychologist who hypnotized me did not ask *any* leading questions.

6. **Careful Examination:** I evaluated the credibility of my memories as I recalled them. I used my skills as a forensic social worker/divorce custody evaluator to interrogate myself. When I spoke (on camera) with experts who don't believe recovered memories are credible, I was not asked any questions that I had not already asked myself multiple times. (Note: Some of these interviews are available on my website and included in my personal documentary *Am I Crazy? My Journey to Determine if My Memories Are True.*)

7. **The Reaction of My Perpetrators:** None of my abusers reacted with love. In the movie "All the Pretty Horses," the female lead says, "I never knew

my father could quit loving me." That's how I felt when I was first remembering non-sexual abuse and respectfully asked my father to go to a counselor with me. His replies were "Is this going to lead you to think I sexually abused you?" and "I won't be seeing you again."

My father

8. **<u>Corroboration from Continuous Childhood Memories:</u>** I have always remembered my father's telling me that he was sexually attracted to me. When I was a teenager, my mother told me multiple times that her legs look better than mine.

9. **<u>A Happy Life Now</u>**: I have continued to grow more and more emotionally healthy.

10. **<u>Spirituality</u>**: The memories came from God. There is a small, still voice within my deepest self that tells me that I now know the truth of my childhood. I like to believe that this alone would be enough to convince me of the validity of my memories.

27

Family

My True Family

I like to have lots of contact with the people who I care about. During the pandemic, I started hosting online cousin reunions. Everyone came, everyone enjoyed it, and everyone appreciated my orchestrating it. In fact, they apparently thought I did such a good job hosting that no one else offered to host. I anticipate being the host of the cousin reunions for as long as I live, which is okay with me. I love doing it. In addition, I get a thank-you note from a cousin nicknamed Bunny after each meeting.

I have no biological ties to these cousins. They are my husband's relatives. I believe a family is a group of people who love and support each other.

It is hard to get away from an abusive family, and, for many survivors, it is hard to stay away. We are pack animals. We need others to survive. Yet, I have found a way to thrive without my family of origin.

Let me introduce you to the members of my true family. I have a wonderful husband named Jerry. He and I met late in life, in 2009. We married in 2010. We are happy together—

though not every minute of every day, of course. We have the usual arguments. I am messy, and he is neat. I cook, and he cleans. He thinks he knows the only right way to load a dishwasher, and I strongly disagree. Since he almost always cleans the kitchen, he loads the dishwasher his way. We are a good pair in every way—soulmates.

Our fifth wedding anniversary

We have six biological grandchildren. I have two adult sons, and each of them have three children. Our grand-children all were born after we married. Thus, we became grandparents together. Four are boys, and two are girls. Jerry gets to be a grandfather without ever being a father!

In addition, we have six bonus grandchildren. We are respite foster parents. That means that children who are in foster care come to visit us when their full-time foster parents take a break. (Foster parents are allowed two nights off each month.) We have four boys who I call our "regulars," since they come consistently. These little guys come one at a time so that we can give them lots of individual attention. Using my mother's recipes, I teach them to bake blueberry muffins and bread and to make chocolate frosting. My husband Jerry plays ball and rides bikes with the boys. He helped one child build what has got to be the biggest lemonade stand in the world.

Kaden

I am not permitted to identify children who are in foster care by name, but Kaden is no longer in care. He has been reunited with his biological mother. The first week that Kaden was back at home, he told his mother, "I still want to do respite." She had no idea what this meant, but, like all good mothers, she wanted to do as he asked. When Kaden's mother found out about us, she immediately agreed to let him continue seeing us once a month. Foster parents are not the only parents who need a break! Kaden since has moved out of state, but each summer, we fly him in to see us for two weeks.

My husband and I were foster parents throughout the pandemic. We got our COVID vaccinations as soon as we were eligible for them. Shortly after we were vaccinated, one of the other boys returned home to his biological parents. However, the family situation was far from perfect. (He is now back in foster care.) I was worried about this child and so sad. In that moment, I realized that—in order for me have the emotional stamina necessary to continue to provide care for children who are in foster care—I needed to interact with other children as well. I wanted to also care for a child whose home life was good. I wrote an ad using the words "Grandma for Hire" and got many responses. All our "regular" foster children are boys, so I decided on two little girls. Each is an only child with extremely devoted parents. I babysit Gaebe, age five, weekly. She loves to play in our backyard. I get her library books, and, if I find one we both really like, we go to the bookstore and purchase it. The other little girl, Ella, is a baby, just ten months old. I take care of her as needed. Ella is an old soul. She loves to sit on my lap and watch Beatles music videos.

Gabee dressed up for St. Patrick's Day

I didn't set out to do this, but, one day, I realized that I now have six bonus grandchildren—four boys and two girls. I also have six biological grandchildren—four boys and two girls.

My Cousins and Aunt

My relationships with many of my biological relatives changed in 1993, when I was thirty-seven years old. That is when I recovered memories of my own generational and ritualistic child abuse. Something that helped me immensely during this time is the fact that I have four cousins and an aunt with recovered memories like mine. These relatives did not tell me about their own memories except when they were asked to do so. They confirmed my memories upon my request.

I will refer to my father's brother's daughter by the fictitious name of Katie. I use fictitious names, or no names at all, throughout this essay to protect the identities of my biological relatives. Katie was the first cousin to remember her abuse. In 1984, nine years before I remembered my own abuse, my parents told me that my cousin Katie recalled that she was sexually abused by her father (my uncle). My parents asked me to talk to Katie. They said that they trusted me to determine if her memories were true. I was a social worker with a graduate degree, and the only family member working as a mental health professional. I traveled to Katie's hometown to talk to her about her recovered memories. I had just become a mother, and I brought my infant son with me. I sat with Katie on an old, faded couch. I breastfed my son while I listened to her heartfelt recollections. When she finished, I told her that I believed her. Her face fell. Those clearly were not the words she wanted to hear. She wanted me to say that she was wrong. No one wants to believe that their own father molested them. My parents called as soon as I got back from the trip.

When I told my father that I believed my cousin, he sent a letter to his brother. I have a copy of this letter. My uncle, a minister, had been telling people that Katie should be automatically discounted because she no longer attended church. My father advised my uncle, "Try to find someone who will listen to you and Katie with equal respect, to what each of you may say, and resolve your differences for your soul's sake." This is interesting because nine years later, when I called my father to tell him about my memories suggesting abuse by him, he refused to go to counseling with me. Not even to one session.

In 1988, I moved to the same city where Katie lived. We met for lunch at a restaurant close to where she worked. She told me about abuse by other relatives, such as our grandfather, and I did not want to hear about it. Sadly, although I never quit believing Katie was a victim of father-daughter incest, I broke contact with her. I was not ready to handle the implications of other relatives' being child abusers. I did not see her again for five years.

In 1993, my father's sister courageously told my parents about her recovered memories. My parents immediately discounted her. They said, "She's crazy. We won't ever talk to her again." I called my aunt, and she agreed to meet with me. She did not tell me that I had been abused, but she said that I had witnessed the abuse of other children. I immediately knew that what she was saying was true. Unlike five years earlier, when Katie tried to talk to me, I was ready to look within myself. Three months later, my first memories of abuse surfaced rapidly. I always will be thankful for the kindness shown by my aunt and cousins as I was remembering. One morning, after I remembered something horrific, I called Katie. She was at work, but I knew that she had been at the family gathering where this atrocity happened. I could not wait to talk to her. She confirmed the memory. I was alone in my room, and yet Katie's compassion made me feel like I was being hugged and rocked.

In about 1995, a couple of years after I remembered my abuse, I traveled by myself to see another cousin, who I will call Betty. I stayed with Betty and her family. She had remembered her abuse several years before I remembered mine, and she gave me helpful ideas about how to handle the memories. We connected deeply. At the end of the visit, we stood in the airport saying goodbye, tears streaming down our faces.

A few years later, my relationships with my relatives who had memories like mine became strained due to a difference of opinion. They started trusting someone who raped me when I was a child, even though my cousins acknowledged that he also raped them. They thought that he had changed and that it was okay for him to care for children. I was the only one who spoke out about the insanity of allowing a known pedophile access to children. Some of the relatives chose to end contact with me. I had only sporadic contact with others.

In 2011, I received an email from my cousin Betty. She had heard "fourth hand" that I had made one of my screenplays into the movie *Sister Mary's Angel*. Betty had lots of questions on filmmaking. We were in ongoing email contact until 2013, when I decided to go public about my abuse in my documentary *Am I Crazy? My Journey to Determine if My Memories Are True.* Betty said that she was not trying to silence me, but she had concerns about my making a "public film." I tried to explain that my main motivation for going public was to help other survivors. Betty expressed concerns that her identity and the identities of our other relatives would be revealed. She said that if I made this film,

34

I would be "re-victimizing victims." I tried to reason with her. I said that none of us are famous, and therefore, no one would take the time to do an investigation like that. I broke contact with Betty. As I reviewed our email correspondence in preparation for writing this essay, I realized that if I had valued contact with Betty more than helping survivors who I may not know through film, I would have quit production. In one of my emails to Betty, I said that I doubted the film would ever be widely viewed. I was wrong. My film has been seen by far more people than I ever would have anticipated. It is on two YouTube channels in addition to mine and has more than one million views in total.

All survivors seem to have at least one relative that does not want them to speak out. My film premiered in 2017, in the midst of the #MeToo movement.

My aunt and other cousins refused to give me contact information for a cousin who I will call Lisa. I had been out of contact with her for many years. Her last name had changed, and I did not know her new name. I searched for her on the Internet for over a year before giving up on ever finding her. Then, in late 2014, I went to a three-day conference for survivors of child abuse. Lisa came up to me on the last day of the conference and called me by name. I did not recognize her. I said, "I'm sorry. I can't place you. Did we meet before at a previous conference?" When she told me who she was, I recognized the family resemblance. I was glad to see her! We sat and talked for an hour. Lisa told me she had been there for the whole conference and thought that I had been purposely ignoring her. She said that we had passed in the hallways several times.

Upon request, Lisa gave me her email address. I wrote it down incorrectly. I wrote several emails to her and, when I received no replies, thought that she was ignoring me. Thankfully, things worked out when we saw each other at the same conference the next year. I nervously asked her if she would be willing to be interviewed on film about her abuse as a child for my documentary. She agreed.

I immediately called my cinematographer. He was available and arrived the last day of the conference. Lisa looked nervous when she appeared for the film shoot, but she did very well. She was articulate and authentic.

My first on-camera question was "were you sexually abused by our grandfather?" She acknowledged that she had been, which is the answer I expected. Her answer to my next question was surprising, and the effect it had on me was even more of a surprise. "Did my father ever sexually abuse you?" I could feel my heart beating faster when she said "yes." My other cousins had not been abused by my father. Lisa haltingly said, "He was not somebody who physically touched me, but almost coaching others, somehow. Taking pictures as well." She took a breath, then added, "Encouraging others to be involved in sexual acts with me and filming them."

I had never before talked to an adult who was victimized by my father in child pornography, or in any other way. I had healed enough to know that I should not feel guilty. Nevertheless, I felt bad for Lisa and for the little girl I used to be. As a child, I was made to watch while my father sexually and physically abused little boys and little girls. I was not allowed to talk to the other child victims. I never got to offer them comfort, not with words or kindness. My on-camera interactions with Lisa were therapeutic for me.

I did not have Lisa sign a standard release form prior to the film shoot. I told her that she could look at the footage and decide what portions, if any, I could use. I traveled to her hometown multiple times. We went out to dinner and annoyed more than one waiter by staying at our table for hours. I was disappointed when Lisa decided not to let me use her image or her voice. Soon, I had the idea of hiring a voice actor and using her exact words. She was glad we could make an agreement that worked for her and for my film. I continue to have occasional email contact with Lisa.

My Parents

My parents are deceased. It feels wrong to write about my mother and father, and wrong to leave them out. This essay is about my family, and that is not what my parents are to me. Today is my sixty-sixth birthday. I was born to them, but they are not parents to me. Maybe they never were. I see fathering as ultimate protectiveness, fierce love, selfless devotion. I see mothering as endless nurturing, comfort that rocks you to sleep when you are weary. I have discovered ways to protect, nurture, and comfort myself. I love myself fiercely. And I am mothered and fathered by God.

My father acknowledged that he was abused as a child. Several years before my own memories of abuse resurfaced, my father's sister told me that my father had been sexually abused by a scout master (not the Boy Scouts of America, but a similar group). I was on the telephone with my parents when my father confirmed that he had experienced this abuse. My mother was shocked. I do not know why my father had never told her about this. He had told her that, as a young child, he was fondled by a female teenage babysitter.

Some people say that you have to forgive your parents and other perpetrators. They say that is the only way to heal. I do not know whether I have forgiven my parents. I am no longer angry at them. I am neither afraid of them nor attached to them. I have gotten to the acceptance phase of the grief process. I had to go through emotional hell to get there. I was on camera when I completed the grief process related to my father. My personal documentary *Am I Crazy? My Journey* contains highly charged emotional footage of me talking to my deceased parents while sitting on their graves. Viewers can interpret for themselves what occurred at the cemetery. After viewing my film, every single person who has told me that forgiveness is essential says that they believe I have forgiven my parents.

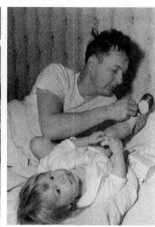

My father

It was harder to grieve my mother than my father, even though I was sexually abused by both of them. I broke contact with them in 1993, shortly after remembering my abuse. I was hurt by the fact that they seemed more interested in continuing contact with my children than with me. They did not acknowledge my birthday in any way, but they continued to send birthday cards to my children, sometimes including a $100 check (which was never cashed). In 1995, I had a goodbye ceremony for my parents at the suggestion of my psychologist. I remember coming into her office to prepare for it emotionally. I said, "I don't think I can do this. I don't think I can live without my mother." I had been estranged from my mother for two years at that point.

Refusing to say goodbye made no sense, but I am sure those of you who have needed to sever your most primal attachment will understand.

My mother

My mother died in a car accident in 1996. I was informed of, but did not attend, the funeral. I do not regret my decision. I had a memorial service for her at my own church. Many of my friends came. My younger son was there, even though his father was not. My first husband refused to attend my mother's memorial service. I was surprised at how much grieving I did the first year after my mother's death. Losing your mother is hard, no matter the circumstances. But as the years went by, I got to a point where I did not think of her often. Then, in 2003, I realized I needed to leave my twenty-three-year marriage. I finally recognized my marital relationship as a type of domestic violence. My now ex-husband had been verbally abusive.

I got strength from a surprising source. Within weeks after I moved out of our 2,900-square-foot home and into a small, rented room, my mother appeared to me in a sort of vision. She had been dead for seven years. She wanted me to confront my father.

Ten days later, I was halfway across the country. I did not know if my father would be in town. I decided to go to his church. Even if he was not there, his reputation would be, and that mattered to him more than anything. When you are not who you say you are, looking good is everything.

When I was in my father's town, I found out that I might have a chance to visit my sixteen-year-old niece, Rachel. However, I then would not have time to visit my father, and I decided to call him instead. I called my father and said everything I wanted to say to him. More than once, loudly and with strength, I said, "You are a pedophile." I added, "You don't want me to tell what you did to me because there will be parents of young children at church who will believe me, and you won't have access to as many children." It was so empowering for me to be unafraid and bold while hearing fear in my father's voice. He was afraid that I would come to his church.

My father pointed out that my siblings allow him to babysit for their children. I said, "It's hard to leave a multi-millionaire father. The only good thing I ever got from you was money."

I stopped the conversation when I was ready to do so. My father was glad for the phone call to end, but he did not hang up on me.

Two days before I left on this trip, I was in my attorney's office working out the final details for my divorce. I asked my attorney if I might be sued for slander. He replied with a phrase that I repeated multiple times to my father. "Truth is an absolute defense."

My father and I had virtually no contact after my mother died, but he called me during the summer of 2005. He told me that he had disinherited me. My reaction was fairly neutral at first. Later I realized how very happy it made me. I would be smiling while stopped at a stop light. I would ask myself why I was blissful, and then realize it was because I had been disinherited by my pedophile father. I spoke to my father for the last time on Father's Day of 2006. I called him and thanked him for disinheriting me. It was an odd phone call in that he started asking some random questions, as though we were having an everyday conversation. My father died of a heart attack in November of 2006. I was not informed of his death at that time. One of my brothers called me in January 2007 to tell me. The attorney for the estate had instructed him to tell me about the will. My brother was surprised that I was aware that I had been disinherited by our multimillionaire father. When I read the will, though, I was hurt. My father left the interest on his money to my siblings, but the principal was put in a trust fund for his grandchildren, minus my sons. My father knew how to hurt me.

My Siblings and Their Children

I have four living siblings—a sister and three brothers. I love them, but they refuse to have any contact with me. They have family reunions, to which I am not invited. My siblings say that we had good parents. The explanation my brothers and sister give for my disclosures is that I am "crazy." Some people have asked me if my siblings were just unaware of my abuse. They definitely were aware. I saw our parents abuse my siblings, and they witnessed my abuse.

I used to feel sadness and rejection over the loss of my siblings. Now I remember happy times together, and I am content. I doubt that I will ever see them again. If I do, I will be comfortable with the life that I have lived and the choices that I have made.

My little sister lived in the same city as my father. As I prepared for my 2003 trip to confront my father, I knew that I could not go there without at least trying to see my sister and her daughter, who I will call Tabitha. I was fifteen years old when my parents adopted my little sister. She was a few months old when we met her. She was a strikingly beautiful baby, with huge blue eyes. I saw her daughter Tabitha for the first time at about the same age. It was like going back in time. My sister and her daughter looked exactly alike as babies. I decided to go to my sister's church.

I made a photo album for my sister and her daughter Tabitha. I did it, at first, as a way to let other people in the church know there is no valid reason for our estrangement. However, as I kept working on the album, it became a work of love. I included a picture of our mother taken when she was eleven or twelve. That's how old Tabitha was.

I saw my niece in the hallway of the church. I thought that I would need to show Tabitha pictures to explain who I was, but she recognized me *and* was glad to see me. What a surprise! My sister, siblings, and parents had not seen a need to brainwash her about me. They had apparently been telling her that I did not want to see her. Tabitha looked through the photo album. She excitedly told me that her cousin, my niece who I will call Rachel, age sixteen, had just moved to the area. Tabitha looked up at me and said, "Have you seen my mom yet? She'll be glad to see you?" I thought, "I doubt it."

As it turned out, we both were right. For the first few minutes, or maybe it was just a couple of seconds, my sister was genuinely glad to see me. Her eyes filled with tears. She hugged me. She let me sit beside her in the adult Bible class, but she quickly showed by her body language that she wanted to distance herself. She left for a while. She must have spoken to my niece. I saw my niece just a few minutes later, and her attitude toward me had changed completely. She seemed to be afraid of me. I later learned that my sister told people that I tried to kidnap her daughter that day. The allegation is ridiculous.

I now had enough information to find my sixteen-year-old niece Rachel. As a teenager, she should know that my parents raped me in case something like that had happened to her. (I did not disclose to my eleven-year-old niece.)

While driving toward the town where Rachel lived, I realized my quickly devised plan would not work. I could not just show up at my brother's front door. I stopped at a Denny's restaurant and used the pay phone to call my niece. When Rachel said hello to me, I talked to her about general things, like her recent move and what she liked about school. When I told her why I was out of contact with my relatives, she changed the subject, but she still heard me. Now Rachel knows she has an aunt who will listen if she was abused and wants to disclose.

I recently reevaluated whether I was right to disclose to this niece when she was just sixteen years old. Back then, it was so painful for me to know my abusive parents had access to children I cared about. I am sorry that I made an opposite decision at about the same time. My ex-husband did business with a couple who had a teenaged daughter who I will call Daisy. During my first marriage, Daisy's parents were family friends. I was uncomfortable with the way Daisy was treated by her stepfather. I recently got back in contact with Daisy's mother. She told me Daisy had been raped by her stepfather just a few months after I left my first marriage. I called Daisy and apologized for not doing or saying more when I saw signs of her being groomed by her stepfather. How can this apology be sincere if I believe my call to Rachel was wrong?

My Sons

I will not say anything identifying about my two grown sons, but I will say that they both are doing well professionally. They are good fathers, which is what is most important to me. I am certain that I will never quit loving them, no matter what happens in the future.

Although I am careful to limit what I say about my sons, to write a memoir, I need to include my deepest pain and most difficult struggle. My sons refuse to talk about my childhood, but they will talk to me about other things. Their actions indicate that they do not believe that I was abused as a child. When they were children, they wholeheartedly believed me. They knew that their father at times indicated that he did not believe that I had been abused. Of their own accord, when I went into their room to pray with them before bedtime, their own words were, "Dear God, please help my dad to start believing my mom." When my older son was eleven and started staying home alone for short periods, he told me, without being coached, that he would call the police if my parents showed up at our door. He would tell the police, "These people hurt children." When he was twelve, he was angry at me because I chose not to initiate any court action against my parents. He said, "If you don't sue them, you are just letting them get away with it."

Recently, I was a research subject for a doctorate student. I was interviewed about my childhood abuse. In answer to her questions, I told her in detail about multiple incidences of the most extreme child abuse imaginable. Then I was asked this question: "Think about the event you consider the worst event, which for this questionnaire means the event that currently bothers you the most. Briefly describe the worst event." My immediate answer was, "My sons being told bad things about me by my siblings and my ex-husband."

My sons and their children attend family reunions that are arranged by my siblings, as do my ex-husband and his wife. My sons seem to make a point of not telling me about these reunions, possibly to spare my feelings. Nevertheless, I always do find out about them, often at inopportune times. The last time that I found out about one was while at my youngest grandson's birthday party. I was surrounded by young birthday guests and their parents. I was careful not to show my pain outwardly. Fortunately, I needed to retrieve the birthday goodies from my car. I walked out to my car, got in, and sat there, all alone. I did not cry, but I concentrated on each breath, in and out, until I calmed down. I reminded myself to stay present. After all, I otherwise had a wonderful day. My son knows that I love to bake, and he let me bring the cupcakes for the party. I had so much fun doing this! My grandson loves cats, and I felt rich buying all the cat-like decorations Walmart had in stock. After fifteen minutes alone in my car, I was able to go back and enjoy the magic of singing "Happy Birthday" and blowing out candles.

My sons do not allow me to babysit. They have never told me their reason. Recently, I found out inadvertently from a source I choose not to name. My sons do not want me to inform their children of my "trauma." Yes, it occurs to me that they could have just asked me not to talk to their children about my childhood.

I am unwilling to change the course of my own life for someone else's secret. It is possible that my grandchildren will read this memoir or see one of my films, all of which are readily available on the Internet. I will never disclose to them personally, however. "Ask your father" will be my only answer if my grandchildren ask questions about my childhood abuse. I have read that it is easier on the children if the secret keeper is the one who eventually discloses.

I may never babysit my grandchildren, but I have a good relationship with each of them. And I have six bonus grandchildren who often do stay in my home.

When my husband and I applied to be foster parents, there were complications and delays caused by my sons. We applied through a private agency. Like many Washington State foster parents, we went through a private foster-care agency rather than working directly with the state, since private agencies are known to offer an additional level of responsiveness to the needs of foster parents and the children in their care. From the time I filled out the initial application form, I had been up front about that fact my sons did not allow me to babysit. At the time, I could not explain the reason. By state mandate, the foster-parent evaluation process requires that all adult children be interviewed as references. During our last home visit, after the social worker had talked to my sons, I was asked questions that cause me to believe the social worker had been informed of the ludicrous allegation that I tried to kidnap Tabitha, my sister's daughter. My explanations must have been satisfactory because the agency approved us.

The next step in the process was for the state of Washington to approve the home study submitted by the private agency. One day, I got a call from our social worker with the private agency. I assumed it was to tell us that we had received approval from the state. (We had already heard of an urgent need for a week-long respite stay of a teenager.) Instead, I was told that the state of Washington was unable to approve us because our home study stated that we were not allowed to babysit our grandchildren without giving a reason why. Under open-records law, I had the right to read the home study, which potentially could have given me the information my sons did not want me to have. I pled with my sons through email to grant permission for our private agency to include the reason in the home study report. I received no reply. I had the idea to waive my legal right to view the report. This worked. My husband and I signed a document waiving our legal rights to open records. The private agency was transparent in its report. The state of Washington was informed of all details about the investigation, including what my sons said about why I am not allowed to babysit my grandchildren. Clearly, the stated reason did not include allegations of abuse. We were approved by the state in time for the young man to stay with us while his foster parents, who had not taken any breaks in two years, took a one-week cruise.

Before becoming a foster parent, if I had been given a choice between being allowed to babysit my grandchildren or being a foster mother, I would have chosen the former. Now that I've been a foster mother, it would be an easy choice. I would choose fostering. I am not choosing my foster children over my grandchildren. I am simply choosing the very full life I now have, with twelve grandchildren—six biological and six bonus. My foster children are grandchildren to me, and so are the little girls I babysit. When Gaebe started kindergarten, she needed two emergency contacts for school. Her mother was thrilled when I agreed to be one of them. And Ella's mother, a nurse, calls me "an angel" when I am able to respond to her last-minute childcare requests.

I love my sons, and I know they love me. I trust them. For medical emergencies, I have designated one of them as my health-care representative in case both my husband

Jerry and I become incapacitated. My other son is the executor of my will if Jerry is no longer alive when I die. Since I am including only necessary information about them, I cannot tell you about all of their many wonderful accomplishments. I cannot explain how personable they are. What I can say is that I am proud of my sons.

More than one person has told me that they think my life would be different if I had daughters instead of sons. They think daughters would more likely believe my account of my childhood. I do not know whether that is true or not, but I do think I would spend more time on the phone with them. My sons call me, but not as often as I would like, and the calls are shorter than I would prefer. I do not think this complaint has anything to do with being a survivor of abuse. Many, if not most, mothers of adult sons would say the same thing about their phone conversations.

My Family Relationships Now

After my sons were born, I did think about adopting a daughter. I probably would have done so had my first marriage been a happy one. The day that I started writing this essay, a young woman named Melanie contacted me through Facebook. She asked for advice about separating emotionally from her abusive mother. Knowing I could not give a short answer to this question, I set up a phone call. While walking in the woods on my favorite path, I talked to Melanie for ninety minutes. She appreciated the advice I gave her. I listened as she told me about her life, and she showed interest in mine. She thanked me profusely for the call. If I had adopted a little girl, she would be a grown woman by now and almost exactly the same age as Melanie. The very next weekend, I was contacted by Marly, who is just one year younger than Melanie. Marly had seen my film and had questions for me. I scheduled the phone call so I could talk while walking on the same wooded trail. We talked from the time I left my house to the time I returned to it. It was during this phone call that I realized I do have daughters, and they like talking to me on the phone!

At our last cousin reunion, there was a discussion that helped me put things in perspective. My husband and I listened as one of our cousins talked about the birth of his first grandchild. Our cousin Bunny spoke up. She warned the new grandfather about the upcoming changes to his life. Bunny and her husband used to babysit for their grandchildren three days a week, which is more than they considered ideal. Bunny said they now babysit only occasionally. However, they are concerned that this could change soon, since their daughter is taking on a more demanding work schedule and might need more help again.

I have children in my life for exactly the amount of time that I want. I can say no to babysitting the little girls. We have the option of declining respite foster care requests. I have time alone with my husband, time with children, and a good relationship with my sons and grandchildren. I have family.

My Parents Were KKK Members and Pedophiles

Trigger Warning: Extremely High

When I watch video of an arrogant police officer with skin the color of mine kneeling on the neck of a Black man pleading for his life, I see the squinting eyes and the "I have the right to take your life," contorted face of my father.

I struggle with how to process my personal experience in the context of the racial justice conversations in which Black voices should be primary. Do I have the right to speak out? Do I have the responsibility to do so?

My parents were in the Ku Klux Klan. To hide their KKK membership, my family led a double life. My paternal grandparents proudly displayed the plaque that they received for their work while on the board of directors of a Black Christian college in Terrell, Texas. My father, a spirited singer, often was asked to be the guest song leader for the gospel meetings held by a Black Church of Christ in Seattle, Washington. Occasionally, he was asked to lead singing at other area churches, always ones whose members were predominantly, or exclusively, Black. My parents taught me to say "Black" when it replaced "Negro" as the preferred term. *Eeny Meeny Miny Moe* involved catching a *tiger* by the toe. I never heard either of my parents use a racial slur.

My parents

I now believe that my relatives had a sinister reason for working so hard at appearing nonracist; it made it easier for them to get away with victimizing Black people. As a teenager, I was obsessed with reading books like *Manchild in the Promised Land* and *Black Like Me.* My cousins, all of whom are as pale as me, passionately discussed these books with me.

My first memories of childhood abuse surfaced in 1993, when I was thirty-seven years old. Even as a child, I had no conscious memory of the abuse, except for being aware while it was happening. By 1993, three of my cousins had remembered ritualistic abuse. Since accusations of fabricating memories were common in the 1990s, we decided to be

51

careful. My cousins shared the details of their memories only when I sought confirmation for similar ones.

Regaining so many memories in such a short time was exhausting. However, one particular memory came with a tenderness that still touches me as I recall it. I had just gotten home from driving my sons to school. I parked in the garage and turned off the engine. Sitting in silence in my SUV, I heard a love song. Since I had now become accustomed to memories surfacing, I wondered if this song was in some way associated with my childhood abuse. When I asked God about it, there was no message other than His/ Her/Their love for me. I rested one arm on the steering wheel and did not move at all for what seemed like an hour, though it was only fifteen minutes. I felt comforted, relaxed, rested. Then I saw flashes of a white cross.

Next, I remember what, at first, seemed like a Sunday drive. I was eight years old. I had on a pretty dress, white lacy socks, and the shiny shoes that were only for wearing to church. My father drove our Ford station wagon. My mother sat up front with him.

We stopped and picked up the medical doctor we called Dr. D. For most medical problems, I was taken to Group Health, where my father's insurance from his job at Boeing paid for treatment. I was treated by Dr. D when I "fell" too often or had yet another bladder infection.

Dr. D sat in the back seat with me. I stayed on my side of the car. I do not know how far we drove. It seemed like a long way to an eight-year-old. I leaned against the car door and fell asleep.

Somewhere out in the country, we stopped at a shack. A Black man invited us in. He may have been one of Dr. D's patients or someone my parents knew from their church connections

Once inside, my father and Dr. D pulled out their guns.

I saw two women, also Black, both of whom looked older than the man. It is difficult for a child to guess the age of an adult, especially one of a different race. The man was skinnier than the women. My father tied the women to chairs in the kitchen. Boards already painted white were taken out of the station wagon, and a cross was erected inside the shack. The man's arms and legs were strapped to it. There was a little girl who was exactly the same size as me. She was cute, with tiny braids all over her head. Her dress was clean and ironed. I remember thinking that someone must really love her.

One gun was pointed at the little girl's head and the other gun at my head. The man was told that if he would pretend to die willingly, as Jesus did, his little girl would be spared.

My mother held our eight-millimeter camera. I knew that there were people who liked to see movies of murders. I had already been made to lay motionless after beatings and pretend to die on camera. Apparently, people who like to see Black men killed also like to see little white girls with their clothes off. I had to do things to the man while he was on the cross.

I stared at the man's face. He was dead. I do not know whether he died from hanging on the cross or from what they made him eat. I was not left to wonder how the little girl died. As soon as the man took his last breath, my father shot the little girl in the head. The women screamed. I screamed too. Dr. D and my father then moved quickly. They set the shack on fire. My mother tried to grab my hand, but I did not want to leave with the bad people. I wanted to stay with the good people and die. I broke free and ran back into the burning shack. One of the women looked straight at me and said, "Little girl, go so you can grow up and tell what happened."

At my next counseling session after recovering this memory, I carefully read aloud what I had written in my journal about this incident. I was relieved when my counselor thought it might simply be symbolic. I called a cousin later that evening. He said, "I haven't had a memory like that one." I breathed a sigh of relief. Then he said, "The Black men I saw crucified had no family. They were homeless."

For years after this memory surfaced, I was obsessed with trying to spur a murder investigation. My childhood home was near Seattle, Washington, but I did not know where the crime had been committed. I could have been driven to a neighboring state or even to Canada. Still, I contacted police departments in Seattle and surrounding cities. Sometimes I was put on hold, but in the end, I was told that there simply was not enough information for any type of investigation. There is no statute of limitations on murder, but you must at least know the jurisdiction. I considered hiring a private investigator to look for records of the death of a family unit that included a father, a little girl, and two women. However, I realized that they may have been unrelated, homeless individuals who my parents lured to a shack with a promise of food or medical care.

I recalled the eyes of the man whose body I was forced to touch. Was he someone who would pretend to die on a cross willingly even if the child whose life would be spared as a result was not even his own daughter? Was the woman with the kind voice not asking for a favor from me when she said, "Little girl, go so you can grow up and tell what happened?" It occurred to me all these years later that she was not beseeching me to tell her story. She did not want anything from me. She was using her dying breath to plead with me not to give up on my life. With parents so evil as mine, I would need a purpose to go on living. Telling a story is a purpose that even a traumatized little girl can quickly comprehend.

As I continually figure out, my life purpose is to do what I can to make the world a safer place. This desire propelled me to be a social worker for twenty-three years, and it motivates me now to make films that make a difference, to be a foster parent, to write, to share truths, and to heal.

My goal is not to spur an investigation of a crime that occurred almost sixty years ago. My parents are dead. Dr. D is dead. There can be no real justice after the perpetrators die.

My goal in sharing this truth, these atrocities, is to build a slightly less hazardous space so those who suspect their loved ones were killed in a similar manner may speak out, should they choose to do so. But I must admit that even this comes from a mostly selfish desire of my own burdened heart.

There is some logic behind my telling about something that happened so long ago, for it was not an isolated historical event. The KKK is active today, and it is far more dangerous than many people realize. Days after Mr. George Floyd was murdered and I was once again flooded with memories of my father's brutal acts, I posted something about my parents on Facebook. Not even four hours later, I was contacted by two individuals, both with skin the color of mine. One said, "I witnessed the murder and dismemberment of a Black girl when I was eight. The little girl was eight too." The other, a young woman who was sex trafficked as a child by relatives, told me that her mother currently is a KKK member and sex trafficker of minors.

Brave readers, I write about brutal acts because I know that there is no defense against atrocities known only by perpetrators and their victims. I write about this so that those of you with skin the color of mine will get close enough to the burning shack to allow it to illuminate any parts of your heart that you have kept hidden from yourself. Because there is no such thing as being just a little bit racist.

People ask me why my parents and other relatives did such horrible things, as though I am some sort of authority on evil. I concentrate on the things that make a difference to me, like how I can quit feeling guilty about the crimes committed by my parents. And I remind myself that it is mothers who give life, and that when my young body wanted to die, it was given new life by the words of a Black woman.

Sometimes I allow myself to forget that I am white. Otherwise, I see my face when I watch video of Amy Cooper telling a Harvard-educated birdwatcher armed only with dog treats that she will "Call the cops . . . and tell them there is an African American man." When the National Football League commissioner finally acknowledges what have always been the rights of Black NFL players, his voice sounds much too similar to that of my father. When I see video of Mr. Armaud Arbery being gunned down while running, I remember the steadiness with which my mother held the eight-millimeter camera.

With my eyes closed, I am learning how to paint happiness into every corner of my life. Happiness scares me. It was the exotic animal that was brought into my childhood only when it led a parade of torture—my own, and that of people who, in my heart, became more related to me than those who share my blood, my features, my complexion.

And I pray that, before I die, I can live in a society that is reflective of a truth I have known since I was a little girl.

A truth that is both indisputable and, somehow, possible to ignore.

The truth that Black Lives Matter.

My Relationship
with Religion

Trigger Warning: Medium

. . . .

Taken from a sermon given at a Unitarian Universalist Congregation, July 22, 2018.

. . . .

Note: The beliefs of the Unitarian Universalist denomination are inclusive. There is no shared creed. Members are encouraged to do their own "responsible search for truth and meaning," which may lead to the embracing of diverse beliefs, including both Eastern and Western religions and philosophies.

My Spiritual Path

The kid in me jumped at the chance to be in this pulpit. You see, in the Church of Christ, which is the church of my childhood, women are not allowed to preach. I went to church three times a week. As a deeply spiritual child, I came up with tons of ideas for sermons, but I could not use them. I am doing something today that has been on my bucket list most of my life.

I was asked to tell about my current beliefs, explain where I came from religiously, and what, if anything, caused me to change.

Unlike me, my husband Jerry can answer these questions quickly. He would say, "I was born Jewish, and I am still Jewish."

Jerry refers to his father as a Jewish saint. This was a man who, like many men of his era, came home from work to find dinner on the table. However, unlike most men, he went into the kitchen and washed the dishes after he ate. Jerry's mother was a ninety-five-year-old widow near the end of her life when Jerry called to say that he had met someone special. Her question was, "Does she cook for you?" Every time he called her, she asked, "Does she still cook for you?" We took an emergency trip to see her, and she literally, and I mean literally, got up off her death bed to meet me. She took us out to lunch and then went back to bed and died ten days later, secure in the knowledge that her son would not starve.

My Evolving Beliefs

I did not have parents like Jerry's. I left my childhood church because it was the only way I could be sure my children would be safe. The Church of Christ is a close-knit community. I could not find a congregation close to my home that was not in some way connected to a relative or friend of my parents. I had been molested by my parents and by other church leaders. Sacred Christian symbols, such as crosses, were desecrated as a part of the ritualistic child abuse I experienced. I remembered this abuse at age thirty-seven. When I left the Church of Christ, even though it had been many years since I believed only members of the Church of Christ would be saved, I had nightmares about going to hell. I went to several different Christian denominations, and my beliefs became progressively liberal. I came here, to this church, in 2005.

I like to believe that I would have left the Church of Christ anyway. I saw inconsistencies between what the Bible teaches and what was taught in the Church of Christ, which supposedly goes strictly by the Bible. I was an avid Bible student. I read the Bible cover to cover for the first time in seventh grade. I was in about tenth grade when I realized I could find no reasonable explanation for the biblical account of Deborah other than that God had appointed her religious, spiritual, political, and military leader of the Jewish people. In sharp contrast, in my childhood church, women were not eligible for any leadership role.

I believe that there is good in all religions. I believe

that every person has the right to choose their religion. I am reminded of a funny story about my older son when he chose his religion. When I left the Church of Christ and went to a series of other churches, my older son got tired of all the changes. When he was twelve, he asked if he could go to his buddy's Baptist church permanently. I said yes. He would leave early on Sundays to go to church and would not come home until evening. I found out years later from his friend's mother that my son and his friend were not at church all day. She told me that my son hung out after church with her family and even took naps at their house. He fooled me so that he could avoid doing household chores one day a week! My son is still Baptist, but he is a father himself now and has no way to get out of housework on Sundays.

I have been asked how I can believe in God after the life that I have had. I have been angry at God, but I have never quit talking to Him/Her/Them. When my younger son was nine years old and in the car alone with me, he asked why his father had quit going to church the last few weeks. I told him that his father (to whom I was married at the time) was angry at God because of my child abuse. My son said, "But God didn't do it. Your parents did." Most of the fellow survivors who I have met are quite spiritual, each in their own way. Maybe that is because we have needed to be in touch with our child selves in order to heal.

I was sexually abused by a female Sunday school teacher in the Church of Christ, a church that taught that gays would go to hell. What a horrific and confusing experience for the young girl I used to be. Yet, I continued to adhere to the teachings of this church. I remember cooking a meal with a gay friend named Charles. I was in my midtwenties. I am sure that I was trying to convert him because, back then, I was constantly trying to convert people. Charles told me that God approves of his lifestyle and used the biblical story of David and Jonathon as proof. I argued with Charles, but from then on, I could not read those Bible verses without feeling confused. I no longer interpret the Bible literally, but if I did, I would have to say that David and Jonathon had a physical/sexual relationship that was blessed by God. My views on LGBTQ+ issues changed gradually. I am ashamed to say that I was in my forties before I was fully accepting of the people for whom I now have such great respect.

Heaven and Hell

I was taught to believe in heaven and hell. I do not believe in hell anymore, but I do believe in heaven. My belief is that everyone goes to heaven, and that the people who are loving and kind are especially happy there. The good news is that anyone who wants to learn how to love can be taught, even after death. Seven years after she died, my mother started appearing to me as an angel. Even now, I sometimes feel her presence while I cook. I wrote a fictional story in honor of this angel experience. In the heaven of the story, your age when you arrive depends on your spiritual maturity. The character who represents my mother became a cute little seven-year-old angel. She is nurtured in the day-care area of heaven. Eventually, she realizes how her life affected me and demands to go down and fix everything. *Ruby's Heaven* is a mother-daughter story with a seven-year-old mother.

The daughter of one of my friends recently committed suicide. I call this friend on a regular basis. We have uplifting conversations, which is what my friend needs right now. I would not have been able to do this if I still held to my childhood beliefs that suicide condemns one to hell. I can easily listen with compassion as my friend talks about her daughter. I now know that even after suicide, or especially after suicide, the deceased are nurtured until such time that they accept love from God. If that never happens, they are still nurtured throughout eternity.

I am a Unitarian mystic. I believe in heaven because I have been there. My sister Ruth died of brain cancer when I was nine and she was eleven. After I remembered my childhood abuse, I disclosed to close friends. They were compassionate at first, but later, they simply could not handle hearing about this abuse. I felt so very lonely. I was in my living room praying. I asked God to let me see Ruth as she would be now if she had lived. Instead, God brought me to heaven; I was with Ruth and with God and with all that is good. It was beautiful and holy beyond description. It does not matter to me if others believe that I had this experience. I know I did. I cannot describe it. Right after my visit to heaven, when I could still see it clearly in my mind, I tried to find words to describe it. All I could come up with were words like awesome and amazing.

Leaving My Childhood Church

I consider myself a Christian, and yet I do not hold to the most basic Christian belief. I do not believe that someone needed to die for me to have a good relationship with God. I was so severely abused that I can relate to death by crucifixion. Back when I still believed the Bible was the literal word of God, I saw the death of Jesus as a way that he showed he could relate to some of my suffering. However, the Bible does not indicate that Jesus suffered for as many years as I did. I always will call myself a Christian, even though I know many Christians do not accept me as such. I have lost a lot because of my abuse. I see no reason to completely lose my childhood religion.

I call the Church of Christ my childhood church only

because I have not figured out how else to refer to it. I was a member of the Church of Christ until I was thirty-eight years old. I hope you can tell by looking at me that I am not yet seventy-six years old, which means I was a member of the Church of Christ for more than half my life. I am glad I left, but I have recently recognized how much I lost. I unfairly blamed the fact that I did not keep in touch with my Church of Christ friends on their religious beliefs. I now realize that I was simply afraid of rejection by them.

Recently I attended a reunion for York Christian College, the Church of Christ school I graduated from. It had been about thirty years since I had talked to any of my fellow classmates. I was afraid they would reject me because of my new religious views. This would have been painful, since the York dorm was the first place I had lived where I felt accepted.

I was an outcast in high school. Other than trying to convert my fellow classmates to the Church of Christ, I kept to myself. Hardly anyone at high school knew my name. I didn't go to my high school graduation because it was on Wednesday night, which was reserved for the mid-week service at church. I did not date in high school. We were not supposed to marry outside our religion, and my parents made it clear they did not want me to date anyone except a member Church of Christ. I met Church of Christ teenaged boys at youth group, but they did not ask me out on dates. I was pretty. Straight-as-a-board hair like mine was the fashion of the day. My shiny, thick mane almost touched my small waist. I could not figure out why I was so unpopular. I now think I had an "I'm taken" aura as a result of paternal incest.

High school senior picture

At York, there were no outcasts. Each evening, virtually the entire student body gathered around the fountain in the middle of the campus and sang uplifting Christian songs. At curfew time, everyone hugged everyone goodnight. Several of the young men asked me out on dates. I accepted. During the second semester Dave, a premed student, invited me to accompany him on early morning walks. Male students weren't allowed to enter the women's dorm. At 6:45 on weekday mornings, I stepped outside. Dave was always waiting for me, jean clad and smiling. We had long talks about our goals and dreams, some of which came true (Dave is a doctor) and others did not (our relationship ended before our second year of college). The change in me was permanent. I opened up because Dave encouraged me to talk about myself. He listened in a way that made me feel important.

This deep communication with Dave was possible only because of the relationship I had developed with my roommate, Missy. She shared her thoughts and feelings with me, even the ones that other people might keep quiet about. In turn, I confided in her. Reconnecting with Missy through the York reunion was an exciting, and scary, opportunity. She is a member of the Church of Christ congregation she grew up in. I told Missy about my life, and I felt just as accepted as I had during the late-night talks in our dorm room. I told her about the closeness I felt to my deceased sister Ruth during my heaven vision. There was a pause. I thought Missy was offended by my unorthodox spirituality. Then, in her soft, sweet voice, Missy told me that she had a vision of her father shortly after his death. He came to her while she was sleeping and handed her a piece of fruit from heaven: it was the shape and color of a red grape and the size of a plump apple. In her dream, Missy ate the fruit. For the next two days she felt so satisfied and full that she did not want to eat at all. Missy was comforted by seeing her deceased father in much the same way I was comforted by seeing my deceased sister. I felt just as close to Missy as I had when we were roommates.

York College graduation

Another former York classmate expressed her disagreement with my new belief system. Carladean, who has been a missionary in Africa for most of her adult life, suggested things that I could say to my husband to convert him from Judaism to Christianity. I explained that I do not want to do that and that I enjoy synagogue worship services. She let me know that her beliefs differ from mine by saying, "I have friends who are Muslim, but they know I don't believe they will be saved." Based on how I used that phrase when I was in college, I think Carladean believes my husband will go to hell. And yet, Carladean and I continue to be friendly and to attend Zoom college reunions together.

I have patience for the people who try to convert me and/or my husband because I used to focus a huge amount of my time and energy on trying to do the same thing. I remember lying in bed and crying at age seven. I remember it so clearly that I can feel the blankets that were on top of me that night. My tears would not stop. At Bible study that night, I had finally understood what was being taught. None of my grade school classmates went to the Church of Christ. Consequently, they all would go to hell when they died. As a child, a teenager, and an adult, my motive for evangelizing was as pure as the heart of my seven-year-old self. I was just trying to help people. And that is what Carladean and others like her are doing.

What I Believe Now

What are my current religious beliefs? Goodness can never be wrong. Kindness is a complete religion. My beliefs compel me to spend the rest of my life trying to treat other people the way they want to be treated, even though I know I will never be able to do so perfectly.

It saddens me when religious terms and names for

God divide people and keep them from loving each other. I was a substitute teacher for a kindergarten class. It was the first time the teacher had been gone. The kids missed their teacher, and one little boy was especially distraught. All day, while the other kids were calling me Mrs. Knight, he called me Mrs. Black. I did not correct him. I believe God will respond to us lovingly, regardless of what name we call Him/Her/Them.

I want to mention one last religious view as I end this sermon. I believe that women definitely belong in the pulpit.

Epilogue

When my husband Jerry and I moved to Washington State in September of 2018, we joined a synagogue. It is very inclusive and, in that way, reminds me of our Unitarian church. But in many ways, the synagogue services have opened a whole new world to me. Part of the service is conducted in Hebrew. There seems to be a constant stream of new words for me to learn. I love to just sit and listen to the beautiful sounds of their songs and prayers. I do not know what is being said, but I have a sense of being in the presence of holiness. Other times, though, I read the English translation of what is being said, which is something I also love to do.

Jerry and me on our back deck

When we moved to our new community, I had intended to become a member of a church. I anticipated attending the church alone, while staying involved as a couple in activities at the synagogue. I visited several churches. During the long process of trying to find a church home, we developed such close friendships at the synagogue that I quit feeling a need for a church. I still attend Christian services occasionally, mostly on communion Sundays. I started attending Ebenezer Baptist via Zoom during the pandemic, and I do not think that I will ever stop. This Atlanta, Georgia, church is where the funeral of Reverend Martin Luther King Jr. took place. It is referred to as "the freedom church," and the music is wonderful. Oddly, it reminds me of my father's highly spirited manner of leading singing at church.

Child Sexual Abuse in Church Settings:

My Experiences and Recommendations for Prevention

Trigger Warning: Medium

Church leaders tend to be highly respected and trusted by their congregations. They are sought out for spiritual guidance. Therefore, sexual abuse by church leaders is particularly traumatizing.

As a child, I was sexually abused by church leaders, and child pornography was taken of me on church property.

As an adult, my primary profession was that of an investigator. I have a master's degree in social work. I worked as an adoption specialist at three private agencies for a total of more than ten years. I placed more than one hundred children in adoptive homes. I investigated prospective adoptive parents to ensure that they had the appropriate skills and motivation to be good parents. Later, I conducted court-ordered investigations. In divorce cases, judges would appoint me to evaluate any allegations made against a parent. I made recommendations to the court regarding child custody and parenting time in more than four hundred cases. I have provided expert court testimony more than one hundred times.

Investigating Allegations of Sexual Abuse in Churches

Based on my experience, I believe external professional investigations are an essential element in the prevention of child sexual abuse in church settings.

The purpose of this essay is to make churches safer for children. This can be done most effectively from the inside. If you are a church member, please ask the leaders of your church to read this essay. My goal is for it to be read by as many church decision-makers as possible.

The first course of action when there is reason to suspect child abuse should be to call the police. I am proposing that a private external investigation by a qualified professional be done when there is an allegation of child abuse, and the police are unable to be involved. Police may be unable to help for the following reasons:

1. An inconclusive police investigation already has been done. The fact that the police cannot find enough evidence for a conviction does not necessarily mean that the suspect did not commit the crime.

2. The statute of limitations has passed.

3. The only known evidence of the crime is recovered memories. Although a common response to trauma, recovered memories are not given as much credence as continuous memories in criminal proceedings.

When an outside agency is not used, the investigation, if any, usually is conducted by the minister. The reason generally is not because of any specific church policy, but rather by default. Ministers do not have sufficient training or experience for these types of investigations. Seminary education does not include training on investigative work. If ministers do the investigation, it most likely will be the first one that they have done. I know that I did not do as well on my first investigation as I did after years of experience. Also, I never evaluated anyone who I knew personally. This would be considered unprofessional because, without realizing it, I could be biased by my previous knowledge of the person I was questioning. A minister could be accused of handling fact-finding differently for someone who, for example, is highly respected by other church members and/or is a major financial contributor.

I recommend the investigative services of GRACE. The acronym stands for Godly Response to Abuse in Church Environments. This organization was founded by Boz Tchividjian, a retired prosecutor. When Tchividjian prosecuted pedophiles who were active in a church, he found that members often sided with the accused perpetrator rather than with the child victim. GRACE is a nonprofit organization. They charge reasonable fees for their investigative services. I have no connection with GRACE, financial or otherwise.

Here is the description of GRACE's investigative work (taken from their website, www.netgrace.org):

> *"If a thorough investigation by law enforcement isn't legally possible, it can be difficult to ascertain facts and determine next steps, which makes an objective, independent third-party investigation crucial for regaining trust with victims and within*

the faith community. GRACE's investigative section includes multiple former abuse prosecutors as well as law enforcement with expertise in abuse and trauma. Each investigation will get a hand-picked team for maximum relevancy and effectiveness in finding the truth. If needed, the GRACE investigative team will include a multi-disciplined team of experts such as clergy and/or psychologists with expertise in the areas of trauma and abuse."

Regarding financial considerations, a policy of hiring an independent private investigator for allegations of sexual abuse will cost no money unless an allegation is made. On the other hand, not having such a policy in place could lead to a civil lawsuit against the church and its leaders. I believe that if a compassionate and effective child safety policy is in place, the likelihood that an adult survivor (or parents of a survivor of any age) will sue is lessened. As a survivor of child sexual abuse in church settings, my only concern is safety for the children of today.

This essay focuses on ways to prevent sexual abuse in Protestant and other non-Catholic churches. Protocol for making policy changes within the Catholic church is complicated by its extensive hierarchy. For current information about child safety within the Catholic church, I recommend SNAP (Survivor Network of those Abused by Priests, www.snapnetwork.org). Since its founding in 1988, SNAP has helped survivors by offering support and advocacy. I have met survivors who greatly appreciate the education and healing they received through attending SNAP conferences.

Background Checks

Child molesters are attracted to institutions that offer access to children. Most churches now have a policy that requires criminal background checks for anyone who works with children, whether that person is a paid staff member or volunteer. I am in favor of a background check, but it should not be the only safety measure taken. A background check can provide a false sense of security. Fewer than 5 percent of pedophiles are apprehended. In fact, criminal background checks would not have saved me as a child. I know the identities of eight people who raped me when I was a little girl. I have searched their criminal records. None have been arrested for child sexual assault or for any other crime.

More than one church leader has told me that they do not have any pedophiles teaching Sunday school. When I ask how they know this, I am told, "We always do background checks." In the late 1990s, I spoke to a well-meaning, but poorly informed, high-level administrator for a respected denomination. When I pointed out that only a small percentage of pedophiles have been successfully prosecuted, he said, "You've given me something to think about." My goal is to give more people in decision-making positions something to think about.

All church leaders, including board members, should submit to a background check. Also, anyone who has a key to the building should be evaluated. Child pornography that contains religious symbols and/or is made on church property sells at a premium price. Key holders have a form of power that often goes unrecognized.

Not Allowing an Adult to Be Alone with a Child

Not allowing an adult to be alone with a child is a part of most church safety policies. This policy remedies some potentially dangerous situations. I have met both women and men who, as teens, were sexually abused by their youth minister. Had this policy been in place and observed, these crimes against minors might not have been committed. However, the policy of having at least two adults with a child is not a cure-all. When I was a little girl, I was sexually molested by multiple adults in my Sunday school classroom after everyone else had left the building.

Many years ago, I had a concern about a youth minister who worked for a respected denomination. I called this youth minister's supervisor. I found out that the youth minister had been promoted. He was now in charge of hiring and training youth ministers for the entire region. The supervisor thought that I would be relieved to learn about this change. I was not. If a child is raped by a youth minister when the supervisor for the youth minster is present, who is going to believe the child?

Successes and Frustrations Trying to Change Church Policy

As an aerospace engineer, my father, a church leader, had federal top security clearance. He produced child pornography using me and other children. He took some of the photographs on church property.

In 1992, my father was the spokesperson for Bear Valley Church of Christ of Colorado. This church was successfully sued in civil court after one of its employees fondled children during counseling sessions. Ignoring mandatory reporting laws, the church leaders did not inform the police or child protective services about the molestation that took place inside the church building. I was in contact with my parents at that time. Neither of them thought this counselor did anything wrong. That belief did not make sense considering that the church had fired the counselor after concerns were raised about him. I told my parents that I disagreed with them. On August 1, 1992, in *The Denver Post*, my father was quoted as saying, "We feel the mindset in society is prejudiced against the conscientious effort of churches to hire and discipline their employees." Less than a year later, I remembered my own childhood abuse, including being sex trafficked by both of my parents.

The fact that I do not have continuous memories of my childhood abuse made it impossible for me to bring any of my perpetrators to justice. I regained memories of the abuse in 1993, at age thirty-seven. At that time, I had four relatives who recovered memories of the same generational abuse that I had experienced. (Later, another relative recalled these atrocities.) I have attempted to provide all pertinent information to the police on numerous occasions. I have received compassion as a result of some of these calls, but the bottom line is always the same. In the states where I was abused, the statute of limitations has already passed. Even if that were not the case, the police cannot investigate based on my testimony. In some states, recovered memories can be used as a source of evidence, but only if there is verification from a source other than recovered memories. I have verification, but only from other people who have recovered memories. No matter how many people recall the same crimes, their testimony cannot be used.

As a child, I was sexually abused in group settings. There were times when I was one of multiple child victims being abused by one or more adult perpetrators. Some of this abuse took place on church property. I knew other child victims well, since they attended church with their families three times a week, as did I. A man who was abused alongside me as a young boy is now an ordained United Church of Christ/Congregational Church minister. After I remembered witnessing this minister's childhood victimization, I tried to connect with him. He was not only unwilling to talk to me, but he was also defensive and extremely angry. He denied that the abuse had happened and called me "crazy." He threatened me, saying that if I ever came to his church, I would be "taken away in handcuffs." I do not know if he abuses children. I do know that I have an uncomfortable gut feeling about him. I feel a duty to provide his denomination with information about my concerns so that they can investigate.

The United Church of Christ/Congregational Church has refused to do an investigation of this minister that meets any type of professional standard. I have made three overtures to them. The first was in 2003. The last was in 2017. Each time I offered to submit to an evaluation by a trained mental health professional to assess the credibility of my statements. I was willing to provide them the names of my counselors, past and present, and to sign a release so that my counseling records could be reviewed by them. They refused my offers. I was given the impression that, on at least one of these occasions, an administrator with United Church of Christ/Congregational Church talked to the minister in question. It seems that this administrator automatically believed this minister's statements without ever assessing the accuracy of mine. Normal investigative procedure requires that the investigator get information directly from the person making the allegation whenever possible. No attempt was made to interview me.

For my own healing and due to my concern about other children being molested by the people who molested me, I went back to my childhood church in 2001. It is a conservative Church of Christ congregation (a different denomination entirely than the previously mentioned United Church of Christ). I spoke to several people who knew me as a child and still attend that church. I was pleased to see that so many good people are members of my childhood church. I told several people that I was abused by someone who is still a member of that church. Some seemed to believe me. I went back to that church six months later and found out that the man who I named as a child molester had, just one week before, been installed as a church elder (the highest level of authority in this fundamentalist church). On the day of my second visit, there was a ten-minute announcement regarding the need for more Sunday school teachers, "especially since we must have two adults in the classroom since we practice the safe church policy."

I was suspicious of Church of Christ members until I met my now good friend, Church of Christ minister Jimmy Hinton. I was browsing Facebook one day, and I saw an article that he wrote on child safety in churches. I really liked the article and started to share it on my Facebook page. Then I noticed Jimmy's description of himself. I had a strong visceral reaction based on my previous abuse by Church of Christ religious leaders. Even though I felt nervous as I did so, I read more of the many articles Jimmy has written on this subject. Jimmy and I graduated from the same conservative Church of Christ college. After getting a master's degree in divinity, he went on to become the minister of Somerset Church of Christ in Pennsylvania. Jimmy's father recently had retired after having served as the minister of this church for decades. Jimmy was new to his job and new to being a parent when his sister Alex disclosed abuse by their father. Jimmy immediately believed his sister and took the information that she gave him to the police. This disclosure was based on recovered memories. The detective at that police department did what some law enforcement detectives would not do in a recovered memory case: the detective used the fact that this retired minister was currently babysitting young children as her reason for bringing him in for questioning.

During this interrogation, retired minister John Hinton, father of Jimmy and Alex, confessed to sexually abusing more than twenty children. In a matter-of-fact tone, John Hinton told his son Jimmy who his next victim would have been had he not been apprehended. It would have been Jimmy's daughter. She was eighteen months old at that time. Jimmy's daughter never has been abused, thanks to her father's willingness to believe his sister's brave disclosure. John Hinton was convicted of multiple counts of child sexual abuse and probably will spend the rest of his life in prison. In addition to his job as a Church of Christ minister, Jimmy Hinton is devoting his life to making churches safer for children. I could not be more impressed with my fellow child advocate Jimmy Hinton.

During the time that I was attending a Unitarian church, I was asked to present a session at the 2015 Shared Hope International Conference. At that time, this conference was the largest gathering in the world of professionals and volunteers who specialize in the prevention of human trafficking and in helping trafficking survivors. My topic was "Church-Controlled Human Trafficking: What It Is and How to Stop It." While researching for my presentation, I found out about the services offered by GRACE. In the fall of 2015, I asked to speak at a board of directors' meeting at my Unitarian church about my recommendations for improving the church's child-safety policy. My request was ignored.

In March of 2017, a Unitarian minister from a church

across the country was arrested for possession of child pornography. Reverend Ron Robinson had been working for a church in Oklahoma since 2015, but during the prior ten years, he was the executive director for the entire Unitarian Universalist denomination. I read everything available on the Internet about Robinson's crimes. The word I will use to summarize them is "disgusting." Our minister devoted a portion of her Sunday sermon to make an announcement about the disgraced former executive director of our denomination. On that very day, the president of the board of directors asked about scheduling me to speak at an upcoming board meeting. I then could make the child safety presentation that I previously had offered to make.

As I researched for this board presentation, I learned that the Unitarian Universalist denomination has found a partial solution. Not all Christian denominations have a governing body, but the Unitarian Universalist denomination does. The Unitarian Universalist denomination's governing body hires a professional investigator in cases when there are allegations against any of its ministers or religious education directors that law enforcement will not investigate. As I asked in-depth questions about the current investigator, I became convinced that she has the skills, training, and objectivity needed to do unbiased evaluations. She is an experienced professional investigator. While her work does not qualify as an external investigation because she is employed by the denomination, I believe that her unique status enables her to operate effectively. She never has been, and never will be, the supervisor of any of the individuals she interviews. Unfortunately, the Unitarian Universalist denomination's governing body does not take any action when an allegation is made against someone other than the minister or the religious education director. If an allegation is made against an unpaid Sunday school teacher or a paid choir leader, for example, the local congregation is not aided by the governing body in handling the situation. Instead, the burden of investigation falls onto the local minister. I asked if local congregations would be allowed to hire the investigator used by the governing body and was told that this professional is not available to do investigations of anyone besides ministers and religious education directors. She is not interested in additional work.

Though well prepared, I felt scared as I entered the room where the board meeting was being held. I was aware of how much the frightened little girl I used to be wanted to prevent abuse in churches. I tried to be clear and concise, while also being convincing. My hands trembled as I read the following statement:

> *"Under current policy, if there is an allegation against anyone at our church, the ultimate duty of investigating falls on our minister, M. I do not think M is qualified to do an investigation like this. I say this with all due respect for her. I am glad she is our minister, and I think she fulfills all her duties well. She is an excellent speaker. I have no complaints about her, and I have heard no complaints about her from others. I am not being critical of M. I simply do not think she has the education, training, or experience needed to do the extremely difficult investigative work involved in a child safety allegation.*
>
> *Churches that believe ministers are God's mouthpiece set unrealistic standards for ministers in general. We are Unitarians. We don't believe ministers receive divine assistance that is unavailable to others. We believe ministers can do only what*

training, experience, and education enables them to do. Our current church policy does not reflect that.

I am impressed that the Unitarian denomination has a policy for investigations of allegations made against religious education directors and ministers. A trained, experienced professional performs these investigations. I am asking that our congregation follow the example set by our denomination.

Under the current climate, sexual offenses from years past are being brought forward. There may be some long-time church members who have not yet been accused but will be in the future. We are naive if we think this cannot happen at our church. Sexual offenses from the past are particularly hard to investigate."

I ended my discourse by describing the services offered by GRACE. I think that I expressed myself well, but afterward, I found out that several board members thought that I was asking for some sort of therapeutic help for adult survivors of childhood sexual abuse. I do not understand how what I had said could be so misinterpreted, and yet I immediately provided clarification.

After my presentation, the board of directors decided that no change was needed. They decided that the minister could handle any situation by deciding whether to do her own investigation or to have an outside agency do it. I wrote this email in response:

"I know our minister will take any allegation seriously and do her best to investigate. I don't doubt her good intentions. However, it's a huge problem if a well-meaning person taints the investigation

*by asking just a few questions. Pedophiles are smart
and just ever so good at not getting caught. When
I was doing investigations, I was quite aware of
the order in which I conducted interviews. I knew
I had a better chance at finding out the truth if
the alleged perpetrator had not been tipped off. I
don't see how M could determine whether a situation needed an outside agency without making the
eventual investigation harder to conduct."*

I thought concerns about money might be an issue in
enacting a policy that would require an external investigation. I offered to donate $1,000 of my own money to be
kept in a fund should an investigation ever be warranted. In
the last email I received about this issue, the president of
the board of directors reiterated that they had chosen not
to make any changes to their child safety policy. They were
declining my contribution. She added, "Should we ever find
ourselves in need of your support or expertise in this area,
I know that we can count on you." To me, that is like my
offering to purchase a fire extinguisher for someone else's
home and the homeowner replying, "No thanks. I don't
want you to buy me a fire extinguisher. However, should
our home ever catch on fire, we'll give you a call since we
know you will be glad to help us out."

I moved to the state of Washington and no longer
attend that Unitarian Universalist church. I have many
close friends there, though, and I was reluctant to include
the difficulty that I had communicating with the church
leaders in this essay. I did so because I want you and fellow
child advocates to know what you might be up against if you
suggest that your own church consider making changes to
their child safety policy, especially changes that may require

external investigations by trained, experienced professionals.

I sent a preview copy of this essay to the Unitarian Universalist minister mentioned above. I consider her response
positive. Her reply email follows:

> *"I think one of the factors in not changing our
> policy was your request to use a specific organiza-
> tion—as that organization may or may not still be
> active in 10 or 20 years. I absolutely don't have the
> information and skills to handle an investigation
> like this on my own and would absolutely want to
> work with an outside organization like GRACE.
> With your permission, I'd like to copy your essay
> and keep it with our policy as a reminder of best
> practice."*

Recommendations

To the church leaders and church policy decision-makers reading this essay, I want to say thank you. You care
about children enough to become better informed. That is
a great start. Change is hard, especially when it involves
giving power to another organization. When you suspect
child abuse or neglect, you must inform law enforcement
and child protective services. You have no choice. That is
the only legal course of action.

In cases in which an investigation by law enforcement is
not possible, you do have a choice to make. I recommend a
change to your church policy to specify that GRACE (or a
similar agency in the unlikely event that GRACE closes its
doors) will be hired to investigate.

The three reasons why police may not be able to help:

1. An inconclusive police investigation already has been done.

2. The statute of limitations has passed.

3. The only known evidence of the crime is recovered memories.

I will end by saying that the most important safeguard for children will always be loving, protective parents (unlike my own). No policy takes the place of parents keeping their eyes open, trusting their instincts, and, above all, teaching their children about good and bad touching.

Children are highly vulnerable and precious beyond measure.

Familial Sex Trafficking and Ritualistic Child Abuse

Trigger Warning: Medium

The Reality of Familial Sex Trafficking

In familial sex trafficking, the child victim is controlled by relatives who allow them to be sexually exploited in exchange for something of value. The thing of value is not necessarily money. Familial trafficking is the most clandestine form of human trafficking.

Most people find it hard to believe that parents would pimp their own child, but it is an undeniable fact that some people pimp innocent children. Therefore, it is logical that some pimps use children who are related to them. If people are willing to do something not only so clearly inhumane but also something with huge legal repercussions, they would look for the best way to hide their crime. If they are fertile, they can parent a child and then use that child. The pimp does not need to find a way to fool or coerce the parent. The pimp is the parent. As disgusting as this line of reasoning is, it is logical.

My father

I am making this point because some people discount familial sex trafficking, saying it is too horrific to be real. It is so upsetting, and due to that, people close their eyes to it. We as a society cannot prevent something that we do not even acknowledge.

How common is familial sex trafficking? Insufficient research has been done to give a conclusive answer. One study with a small sample size indicates that familial trafficking accounts for one third of the cases of minors who are sex trafficked. In 2019, Polaris—an organization dedicated to reducing, preventing, and ultimately ending human trafficking and to supporting survivors—provided services to 14,597 survivors of sex trafficking. For sex trafficking survivors of all ages, Polaris hotline statistics show that the second most common recruitment tactic is familial. The first is through a romantic partner.

Child victims come from all socioeconomic backgrounds. Although it is tempting to think that most people who are willing to pimp a relative are poverty stricken, no research is available to indicate a relationship between wealth and familial sex trafficking. Even if research becomes available, there is a danger of it being skewed. Wealthy people likely are better able to conceal this crime than are those with fewer financial resources.

Familial sex trafficking is so hidden that I did not realize I was a survivor of it until I was in my late fifties. I knew what had happened to me, but I did not know that it was considered to be sex trafficking. I did not think that I had a pimp. I had never been kidnapped or homeless. Now I recognize that my parents were my pimps. Many survivors who I meet have gone through a process like mine prior to identifying as survivors of familial sex trafficking.

The Relationship between Familial Sex Trafficking and Ritualistic Child Abuse

I am a survivor of both familial sex trafficking and ritualistic child abuse. Based on my own informal surveys, I estimate that about 50 percent of familial sex trafficking survivors also are survivors of ritualistic child abuse. For this reason, I always include ritualistic abuse in presentations on familial sex trafficking.

Ritualistic abuse and sex trafficking are not synonymous. Many human trafficking survivors never experience ritualistic abuse. However, every ritualistic abuse survivor I know is also a survivor of sex trafficking. Like me, they were prostituted as a child.

Ritual can be defined as a ceremonial act or series of

acts regularly repeated in a set precise manner. There is nothing wrong with a ritual. In fact, rituals often are a part of religious services. When you combine the word *ritual* with *abuse*, the meaning becomes dark. The definition of ritualistic abuse that I use is as follows: physical and/or sexual child abuse and torture involving either multiple child victims or multiple adult perpetrators or both. It often includes the desecration of a sacred symbol. It can include ritualistic murders.

I now am much more likely to refer to myself as a survivor of familial sex trafficking than as a survivor of ritualistic abuse. Unlike ritualistic abuse, I rarely need to define sex trafficking, and no one says that sex trafficking does not exist. On the other hand, many discount the existence of ritualistic abuse.

Personal Stories of Familial Sex Trafficking Survivors

Familial sex trafficking cases do not follow a set pattern. For this reason, I will give a few examples in the form of survivor accounts.

One survivor who asked me to tell her story also asked that her name not be disclosed. I will call her Rosa. Rosa was raised in poverty by her single mother. Rosa told me that she was very good at making tortillas. At age seven, she was hired by a local restaurant owner. This man raped her. Rosa told her mother, and her mother asked him to stop. He did not stop, but he did give her mother money for rent each month. Rosa and I met at a professional conference. She is a registered nurse who is devoting her life to helping undocumented immigrants.

Judge Robert Lung, a district court judge in Colorado, speaks at human trafficking trainings and conferences. He was sexually abused by his father from age five. Later, he was trafficked by his father. Robert's father was a physician and did not need money. Instead, he wanted access to other children. When Robert was fifteen years old, the abuse stopped. Robert was able to block all memory of the abuse between the ages of fifteen and twenty-five. He recovered his memory of the abuse at age twenty-five. Robert's mother did not know about the child abuse and exploitation. She herself was a victim of her husband's violence. As a result of hard work and counseling, Robert and his mother now have a good relationship.

Robert was featured in *Boys Documentary*, a film about boys and men who were sex trafficked. Experts now believe that at least 15 percent of child sex trafficking victims are male. Some estimates range up to 50 percent.

Elisabeth Corey is a single mother with preteen twins. She supports her family by working as a life coach for survivors of abuse. She was raised in an upper middle-class family. When she was two years old, her parents, uncles, and grandparents started sexually abusing her. Elisabeth's father realized that there was money to be made, and he sold her. By the time she was nine, she had given up. She remembers the moment when she realized there was no hope of being saved from a terrible life. In that moment, she made a conscious choice to forget her abuse. Elisabeth's childhood memories started to resurface when she was thirty-eight years old and the mother of two young children.

Like Robert and Elisabeth, I was raised in an upper middle-class family. We looked perfect on the outside. My father was a Boeing aerospace engineer. He also was an excellent photographer. He used me in child pornography, starting as early as age two. My mother was a college-educated homemaker with a degree in home economics. She sewed dresses for me, sometimes using patterns of her own design. But there were times when I was wearing no clothes and I saw men hand money to her.

I do not know why my parents abused me. Perhaps one reason for my own traumatic amnesia was to avoid grappling with this question when I was a child. When I recalled the abuse at age thirty-seven, I was mature enough and educated enough to at least try to wrestle with this question.

Recovered Memories

One way that society silences survivors is to discount their recovered memories, like those of Robert Lung, Elisabeth Corey, and myself. Delayed recall of traumatic events is common in abuse survivors. All memory is fallible. When researchers compare memories recovered in adulthood to continuous memories, they find that recovered memories are at least as likely to be true as are continuous memories.

In my documentary, *Am I Crazy? My Journey to Determine if My Memories Are True,* I interviewed Pamela Freyd, who, with her husband Peter Freyd, founded the False Memory Syndrome Foundation (FMSF). My quest in producing this film at age fifty-seven was to reevaluate the memories that surfaced for me at age thirty-seven. I had believed these memories to be true for twenty years. I thought the best way to truly question myself was to directly question people who, like my deceased parents, say recovered memories are false. I think that Pamela Freyd agreed to be interviewed because she thought that she could convince me that my memories were false.

The goal of the FMSF is to discount the validity of all recovered memories. Most survivors of ritualistic abuse have delayed recall, as do many survivors of familial abuse without ritualistic aspects. The Freyds had the FMSF up and running eighteen months after their daughter, University of Oregon psychology professor Dr. Jennifer Freyd, recalled paternal incest in 1990. They even managed to obtain a 501C nonprofit status for their organization. Pamela and Peter Freyd frantically attempted to discount their daughter's claims. The FMSF closed its doors in 2019, but there is a similar organization still active in the United Kingdom: the British False Memory Syndrome Foundation.

Although not the official FMSF stance, some of their members minimize the impact of child sexual abuse. In *Am I Crazy? My Journey* longtime FMSF advocate Eleanor Goldstein said, "I don't think sexual touch is the horror of all horrors. I think we make a big to-do about nothing." Pamela Freyd and Eleanor Goldstein have coauthored two books.

The Reality of Ritualistic Child Abuse

People my age often associate ritualistic abuse with the McMartin preschool case of the 1980s in which several teachers at the school were accused of abusing hundreds of children. Some cite this case as evidence that ritualistic abuse does not occur. The evidence in the case shows that the adult son of the owner of the McMartin preschool did, in fact, molest children, whereas the other teachers were falsely accused. The case was grossly mishandled by law enforcement and the district attorney. All charges were eventually dropped—even those against the owner's son. Nevertheless, using the McMartin preschool case to disprove all ritualistic abuse is a much greater tragedy than the fact that it was mishandled.

The book *The Witch-Hunt Narrative: Politics, Psychology, and the Sexual Abuse of Children* discusses the McMartin case in detail. It was written by Ross Cheit, an attorney and professor of political science and public policy at Brown

University. It also provides exceptionally well-researched, extensive details of properly handled cases involving verified child sexual abuse in daycare settings. Cheit wrote this book to counter the damage done by the media frenzy about the mishandling of the McMartin case. He does not advocate that children should be automatically believed in legal settings but that children should simply be acknowledged as potentially credible witnesses.

Pamela and Peter Freyd of the FMSF claim that ritualistic abuse does not exist. This is not surprising. As noted above, many survivors of ritualistic abuse have delayed recall. In an interview of mine with Pamela Freyd about an article written by FBI agent Kenneth Lanning, she stated that he totally discounts the existence of ritualistic abuse. She was pleased when I agreed to read Lanning's 1992 *Investigator's Guide to Allegations of "Ritual" Child Abuse*. When I got back to my hotel after my first day of interviewing Pamela, I immediately found the article on the Internet. I was amazed as I read it. Instead of discounting the type of abuse I experienced, he simply calls it by a different name. Lanning does not like the term "ritualistic abuse" and instead uses the term "child sex ring." I have no problem being referred to as a survivor of a child sex ring, and I told Pamela that the next day during the continuation of our interview. I even read aloud portions of the article.

Ross Cheit's *The Witch-Hunt Narrative* includes a detailed discussion of Lanning's *Investigator's Guide*. Cheit explains that it is "misrepresented almost as often as it is cited." Lanning says of Cheit's observation, "I vigorously agree with that." I believe that Lanning would consider Pamela's reference to his article a misrepresentation. (I have made several unsuccessful attempts to contact Lanning.)

To be fair, Lanning does discount claims of widespread ritualistic child abuse. In the conclusion of the above-mentioned article, he writes, "Until hard evidence is obtained and corroborated, the public should not be frightened into believing that babies are being bred and eaten, that 50,000 missing children are being murdered in human sacrifices, or that satanists are taking over America's day care centers or institutions."

As I reviewed the Lanning article to prepare for this essay, I noticed that Lanning discusses the underreporting of child sex trafficking. (Lanning refers to the commercial exploitation of children not as child sex trafficking but as child prostitution, which was an acceptable term when this article was written in 1992.) The following passage is from Lanning's article:

> *"At professional conferences on child sexual abuse, child prostitution is almost never discussed. It is the form of sexual victimization of children most unlike the stereotype of the innocent girl victim . . . child prostitutes and the participants in child sex rings are frequently boys. . . . In a survey by the Los Angeles Times, only 37 percent of those responding thought that child prostitution constituted child sexual abuse (Timnik, 1985). Whether or not it seems fair, when adults and children have sex, the child is always the victim."*

I have heard disclosures by survivors of ritualistic child abuse perpetrated by high level government officials. I have no firsthand personal experience of abuse by politicians. For those who want to further research the topic of child sex rings involving people in authority, I recommend Nick Bryant's *The Franklin Scandal: A Story of Powerbrokers, Child Abuse and Betrayal*. It gives convincing evidence that Police Chief Robert Wadman of Omaha, Nebraska, perpetrated a variety of crimes, including impregnating Alisha Owens, a local high school student, when she was a minor. This book suggests that these crimes were covered up despite FBI involvement in the case. Certainly, justice did not prevail. Police Chief Robert Wadman was not prosecuted. Alisha Owens, who would not recant her testimony regarding the paternity of her child, received a nine- to fifteen-year prison sentence for perjury. This incredibly long prison sentence alone indicates that there was a cover-up. Nick Bryant's research suggests that higher level officials may also have been perpetrators in the Omaha-based child sex ring.

I do not know of any reliable statistics on ritualistic abuse. I know what happened to me. Some people believe ritualistic abuse does not exist. Others believe it is quite common. I used to be in the latter group. I thought there were ritual abusers at every church, at every school, and in every group of people. This belief made it difficult for me to function in society. Now I believe that most people are good, but that there still are ritualistic child abusers.

My personal mission is to describe to others what I personally have experienced. I do not want to focus on statistics. I want to describe these unbelievably bizarre and yet heartbreakingly true experiences in the most credible manner possible. For example, I have witnessed murders. I give detailed accounts of these murders in other essays, which I have labeled with "extremely high" trigger warnings.

There are books about ritualistic abuse that I used to find helpful but no longer recommend. These books invoke fear in me even now, after so many years of recovery. For me, that fear is counterproductive. I like the way this subject is treated in the twentieth anniversary edition of the groundbreaking book *The Courage to Heal* by Ellen Bass and Laura Davis. Basic information about ritualistic abuse is given on page 118 and 119. Near the end of the book, in the chapter titled "Courageous Women," there are seventeen in-depth survivor accounts. The last one is of a survivor of ritualistic abuse referred to as Sheila (pages 510 to 519). She experienced sadistic abuse in the basement of a police station on several occasions. A few police officers ritualistically abused multiple children, including her. Sheila was made to watch as the daughter of one of these police officers was murdered. Since so many police officers were involved, it was possible to hide the crime.

Trickery is often used in ritualistic abuse. As a young adult, I was frightened about getting pulled over by the police, even if traveling under the speed limit. Five years after my first memories of abuse surfaced, I saw a police officer at the entrance to a bridge on a road that I traveled often. There was a line of cars. It seemed that drivers needed to be told personally by the police officer that they could not cross the bridge and would need to turn around. I sat in the line of cars considering the irony in this situation. In that moment, I remembered the cause of my fear of police. I realized that when I was in grade school, I was raped by a man wearing a police uniform. After working through the memory, I decided that he was not even a police officer. The police uniform, even if not authentic, could fool a grade-schooler. My fear of police has subsided. I must admit that it is now not uncommon for me to drive a bit above the speed limit!

Several mental health professionals have told me that the reason they believe ritualistic abuse exists is because they have provided counseling to credible survivors of it. I felt honored when Dr. Bessel Van der Kolk, one of the best-known trauma experts in the world, agreed to be interviewed for my film *Am I Crazy? My Journey* Dr. Van der Kolk, author of *The Body Keeps the Score,* is a psychiatrist, neuroscientist, and memory researcher. I asked him if he believes that ritualistic abuse exists. Dr. Van der Kolk's expression became solemn as he said, "Sadly it does."

How to Recognize a Child Who Is Being Trafficked

I often am asked if there are signs to help identify child victims of familial sex trafficking. My answer is yes . . . sometimes. A fellow survivor and I both led sessions on familial sex trafficking at the same conference. I went to his presentation, and he presented a general list of signs of child abuse. It included withdrawal from friends or usual activities, changes in school performance, depression, sudden loss of confidence, frequent absences from school, self-harm or attempts at suicide, and reluctance to leave school activities to go home. It is a great list. It applies to many situations. It applied to his situation. The school nurse detected his victimization. But for my little girl self, nothing on the list would have been effective in detecting my abuse. I do not blame my school nurse or my teachers or any of the other kind people from my childhood. I blame my highly intelligent, wealthy parents.

I am pleased that we, as a society, have progressed to the point that we now have conferences that specifically address the commercial exploitation of children. I recently was one of three presenters who spoke about familial sex trafficking at a virtual global summit. Two of us were survivors, and the other presenter was a researcher who had interviewed professionals who work with familial sex trafficking survivors.

How can we stop familial sex trafficking if there are no clues? One important way is to listen to adult survivors. The reports of adult survivors *can* protect the children of today. My call to action is something that you just did. Learn more about this type of abuse by listening to adult survivors. By reading this essay, you have done something important. You have listened to me, an adult survivor. There is no defense against the atrocities known only by victims and their per- petrators.

Ritualistic Abuse:

Examples from My Childhood

Trigger Warning: Extremely High

Murders

As a child, I witnessed murders. I tell about the murders of three adults and one child in my essay "My Parents Were KKK Members and Pedophiles." There were ritualistic aspects of that atrocity, including the desecration of a Christian symbol.

Never before have I publicly disclosed the other murder I witnessed. When I was four or five years old, my mother gave birth to a baby at home. To my knowledge, this was her only home birth. I have other siblings, all of whom were born in hospitals. My birth certificate includes the name of the hospital where I was born. There is no official record of the home birth. From the time I was very young, my mother talked about the fact that she almost died when I was three and a half years old. My mother said she stayed at home in bed for a year because she was so sick. I do not believe that my mother was physically ill. I believe that she stayed at home for a year to hide a pregnancy. I witnessed the baby, my younger brother, being castrated and then murdered by my parents. I saw the penis, and I saw the blood. I remember hearing the baby scream and then stop screaming. I cannot prove this happened, but I know it did. Trickery is sometimes used in ritualistic abuse, but in this instance, it was not.

There were also times when I was convinced that I had witnessed murders, when, in fact, they did not actually happen. For example, I was tricked when I was about five years old. I am not sure whether this was shortly before or shortly after my baby brother's murder. I was made to stand outside on our property in the country. My father and one or two other men were at the top of a small hill. I was told to stand at the bottom of the hill. The men were standing behind a handmade wooden table. Although I could not clearly see what they were doing, I could see they had knives.

I was told that they were sacrificing unborn babies. I do not remember whether they said they were sacrificing them to Satan or to God. I was instructed to stand still for what seemed like a very long time. What I remember most vividly about this incident is how much my feet hurt. I was wearing tan saddle oxfords and white socks. As young children often do, I stood on the outer side of one foot, then on the other foot. I squeezed my toes together as tight as I could. I stood on my heels. I tried anything to stop my feet from burning. I was given the impression that hundreds of fetuses were mutilated. When I first remembered this incident, I thought that actual human fetuses were being used. I since have changed my mind. I honestly do not think that I could correctly identify a human fetus even now. From a distance, it would be easy to fool me by using an animal fetus, or possibly even some other part of an animal's body. How hard would it be to fool a preschooler?

My Sister's Funeral

The following is what I consider to be the worst event of my childhood. I had a sister named Ruth who was two years older than me.

Ruth died of brain cancer in a hospital when she was eleven and I was nine. After she died, her body was picked up at the hospital by someone from the funeral home, as is customary. I was brought to my childhood church by my parents in the early hours of the morning on the day of her funeral. My sister's body and a casket were there when I arrived. The ritualistic abuse happened outside, in a treed area on church property.

My sister's body was placed on the ground. My father cut it with a knife. I sobbed as I saw the knife enter her body again and again. I was made to hold the knife and was told to cut her body. For a couple of years after remembering this incident, I felt guilty about it and wondered how my father had been able to get me to cooperate. I finally realized that I had been so used to doing what my father told me to do that I cut my sister's body simply because he commanded me to do so. My father told me that, like him, I was an abuser. Ruth's body was then placed in the coffin. My father put me in the coffin with my sister. Instead of being repulsed by her mutilated body, I was glad to be close to her. She still was my sister. I touched her hair. I was driven to the funeral home while in the casket.

At the funeral home, my father held a hammer. I was told that my sister's head was being crushed, but it might not have been her head. I was a distraught little girl. Another corpse that was already at the funeral home could have been used, or a body part of an animal. If my husband were murdered today, and the same thing happened to his body that happened to Ruth's body, I do not think that I could correctly identify his corpse, or a part of his corpse.

After this long torment, something was placed in my mouth. I was told that it was a piece of my sister's flesh. This was done as a desecration of the Christian sacrament of communion. Only seven years ago, at age sixty, did I realize what actually was placed in the mouth of my grief-stricken nine-year-old self. It was a communion wafer. It was not matzo, which was the kind of bread used for communion by my childhood church. It was the kind of communion wafer used in mainstream Protestant churches, like Methodist and Episcopal. I now believe that my parents were trying to desecrate the Christian act of communion for me in every church that I might someday attend, not just in my childhood denomination. They would have more control over me if I did not have any family besides them, even a church family. Their plan did not work, though. My religious views have changed over the years, but whenever I have an opportunity to do so, I treasure taking communion.

Ruth reading to me

Someone from the funeral home and both of my parents were present throughout this ordeal. I believe that the person from the funeral home was its director, but I am not sure. The mortuary could be used because the person who was present was a pedophile. After that atrocity and prior to the Ruth's funeral, I was made to have oral sex with this man. I have tried to find out the identity of this person. I know the name of the funeral home and have made several calls. I discovered the funeral home does not keep a record of the person who deals with a body prior to a funeral. The death certificate has the name of the person who worked at the mortuary at the time the funeral was officiated.

I did find the name of the man who owned this funeral home at the time of my sister's death. This man also served as its director. I tried to contact him so that I could confront him about the abuse, but, by then, he had retired and moved to Arizona. The mortuary is in Washington, my home state. I was unable to find a telephone number or address for him in Arizona. I talked to a receptionist at the funeral home who knows him. I told her what had happened to me and my sister, and she promised that she would send him a message asking him to call me. She added that, to her knowledge, he is a nice person and would never hurt anyone. He never called back. I do not know how much good it would have done to talk to him anyway. One of his employees, in fact, may have been the abuser, and the director may not have known about the abuse.

My sister Ruth Ramsey (1955–1964)

I have been asked why I have not had my sister's body exhumed to confirm my memory and to bring justice to my parents. One reason is that I simply do not want to do so. It is still her body, and I do not want it disturbed further. In addition, I do not think that I have the legal right. My four living siblings also would have to consent, and they claim to have no memory of abuse by our parents. They inherited our parents' estate. I was disinherited. Furthermore, the only things that I am sure happened to her body involved only soft tissue damage. This type of damage could not be detected even if Ruth's body were exhumed.

Funeral homes are common places for the ritualistic abuse of children. When I told a fellow survivor that I was placed in a coffin, she told me that she was too. She added,

"It's sad how often that happens." She said that she has heard the same account from many other survivors.

Kittens

Another incident that I consider ritualistic involved kittens. At our home in the country, before I was old enough to go to kindergarten, my parents made Ruth and me watch as they slowly killed our kittens. The kittens were killed one at a time. First, my father and mother took turns throwing them like a baseball. The sandpaper-colored shingles on the side of our house shook from being hit so hard. I could feel the impact in my body, as though I were the kitten. Then, the kittens each were grabbed by the neck and dunked in water. I coughed, as though I were choking. Lastly, my father crushed their skulls with a rock. I held my hands to my head and sobbed. Ruth and I were told that if we ever reported our abuse to anyone, the same things that happened to our kittens would happen to us. This was not the only time kittens were killed. Another time a cat and her kittens were hung, one at a time.

I think of my mother as someone who had multiple personalities. It seemed like she was totally unaware of the abuse much of the time. She often would tell houseguests what was supposed to be a story about childhood innocence related to our kittens. In her version of the story, I accidentally suffocated my kittens. I remember hiding them in my little white suitcase. I took them to the building that the previous homeowners had used as a chicken coup but that was now Ruth's and my playhouse. I brought doll clothes with me. I chose a lacy white nightgown with a matching cap for one of the kittens. That kitten moved its head as my tiny fingers tied the ribbons under its chin to keep the cap on. I put a pink dress with a flowered print on another. I did not dress up the boy kittens. I kissed each kitten goodbye as I gently placed it in the little suitcase. I used a box as a stool and stood up on my toes to push the suitcase onto what seemed like a very high shelf. I saw them once afterward, and they looked like they were asleep. They looked happy. I had no context for doing this prior to remembering my abuse. I now believe that I did this not out of childish ignorance but out of full knowledge of the pain the kittens would otherwise endure. Suffocation from lack of oxygen still seems like a less painful way to die than the torture my other kittens experienced.

In 2010, while my husband Jerry and I were planning our wedding, I searched for the perfect kitten. I made at least a dozen trips to the local cat shelter. I would give myself up to an hour to watch the kittens in their cages before picking one out. Then I would ask the attendant to let me hold the one that I chose. I would cuddle the kitten for thirty minutes, or a little less if the cat shelter volunteer absolutely insisted that my time was up. If the kitten cradled itself into my arms, I would come back and visit that kitten another day and do the same thing. Some young cats acted completely differently on subsequent trips, but a calico kitten named Kenya proved herself suitable for my smothering affection. My decision was made on my third trip to see Kenya, which happened to be two days before our wedding. I asked that she be held at the cat shelter for a week. That was against their policy. Policies do not apply to honeymoons, so I asked my husband if we could postpone ours. On the day we were supposed to leave on our honeymoon, we instead made a trip to the animal shelter to adopt Kenya.

Kenya acted more like a dog than a cat. She liked to snuggle with me, which is something we did often. As I lay in my bed or sat in a living room chair, holding Kenya to my chest and feeling our hearts beat in unison, she healed the wounds caused by the deaths of my childhood kittens.

As a child, as a teenager, and throughout most of my adulthood, I was sure that I would never quit missing Ruth. I did not think the sadness of losing her would ever go away, but it has. I smile when I think of her now. I was with Ruth when our kittens died, and I was cuddling Kenya when I fully healed from the tragic loss of the only person in my family of origin whose love I ever fully trusted.

Familial Sex Trafficking:

Examples from My Childhood

Trigger Warning: Extremely High

Age Six: A Vignette

The little girl is six years old. She lives in a house on a hill out in the country. Her parents invite some bad men to come. No one will hear her screams because the closest neighbor is half a mile away. And, anyway, the closest neighbor is a bad man.

The trees have no choice but to hide what happens.

Her father welcomes the men. Her mother takes the money. The little girl wears a dress: a white dress that is soon dirty. Her father hangs a rope from a tree limb. Her mother ties the rope around the little girl's neck. The first man holds the little girl and does icky stuff to her. She hurts, and when he is done, he looks at her as though to say, "You are lucky I don't drop you. You know you'd die if I did." The little girl does know because her parents killed her kittens by hanging them.

The little girl is passed to the next man, and the next, and the next. Each time, she thinks she might get to die. She wants her mother to care about her.

One of the men cuts the rope. The little girl falls to the ground. The rope is still around her neck. Some of the men scoop up dirt and throw it on her. They go to the bathroom on the pile of dirt.

Her father walks the men to their cars. One of the men yells, "You let it go too far. She's going to die. Take care of her." Her father answers in anger, "She's mine. I know what I'm doing."

The little girl can tell that her mother is still close by. She thinks, "If I just know that my mom cares about me, I'll be okay." She pushes the smelly dirt out of her face and looks at her mother. Her mother looks at her as though she is an animal, not a person. Her mother's look hurts her much more than the men had hurt her. The little girl wants to be dead. She holds her breath. She thinks if she holds her breath long enough, she will die, but that does not work. But she is hurt bad. Maybe bad enough to die, she hopes. Then the little girl sees a bright light. In the light, she sees the face of God. The love she had hoped to see in the face of her mother she sees in God's face. She knows that she can stay alive because God is her mother, and He loves her. Her soul comforts her body, and, for a little while, she likes being alive.

Her mother brushes off some of the smelly dirt, picks her up, carries her inside to the bathtub, and washes her hair. She smells good again. Her mother puts her in a bed with pretty sheets and lies down by her. Then her mother touches her in yucky ways. She cries silently.

This time God does not see the little girl. The little girl wonders about this God who sometimes loves and sometimes turns away. She knows there is no one she can trust, except maybe God.

And the only thing the little girl looks forward to is being dead.

Postscript: This story has a happy ending.

Shortly after the incident, and perhaps because of it, at the tender age of six or seven, I had an epiphany. I was outside watching my mother hang clothes on our clothesline. I thought, "I don't have to be like her." From then on, I took comfort knowing that what made my life worth living was the hope of someday getting to be a good mother.

Just last Wednesday, at age sixty-seven, I had another epiphany. I realized that what makes someone a successful parent has nothing to do with how they are treated, or even thought of, by their adult children. I am a good mother based on my own unselfish intentions and actions. I get to be a good mother (and grandmother) every day, which gives the little girl I used to be reason to celebrate.

Rented by the Hour: A Vignette

My parents knew they could not kill me. I was seven years old, and I watched the news on television sometimes. People get in trouble when their little girl dies. The police come out and keep asking questions until they find out who did it. But this man was not my parent. He would just drive away if I quit breathing.

My father

It was just him and me. We were out in the country, surrounded only by weeds and wildflowers. Screaming did no good. When I begged him to stop, he hit me harder.

I never knew his name. I just knew he was killing me. The thought of dying made me neither happy nor sad.

I heard a car drive up. The door opened, then closed. I heard footsteps. I tried to get up so I that could see, but my body sank, a solid pool of pain.

My dad's face looked down at me. I could tell he knew how bad I was hurt. I thought, "Now I can stay alive. My dad doesn't want me to be dead." I smiled inside my head and pretended that my dad cared about me.

Then my dad got that look on his face, the one that bad men get when they see little girls with no clothes on. He touched himself, and I wanted to be dead.

Note: I promised my readers (and myself) that each of my essays would contain an element of hope. I admit that I had to dig deep to include anything positive in this one. Although I did not always connect my reactions to this incident, I realized years ago that watching the news on television was triggering for me. I quit watching. As a result, I am happier, more relaxed, and still informed about the issues that are important to me. I do my own in-depth research when a topic interests me.

A Partial List of Places Where I Was Sex Trafficked as a Child

- Inside my childhood home
- At my grandparents' house
- Outside my childhood home, not far from where my swing set stood
- In the hotel rooms of men who I had never met before
- In the Sunday school classrooms of church buildings
- In the studio of a professional photographer after regular office hours
- At the home of a church member
- In a doctor's office, by the physician who was friends with my parents
- In the basement of a funeral home

The place where I live now is surrounded by beautiful evergreen trees, like the ones that were outside my childhood home. In the evening, as I sink into the lawn chair on my back deck and watch the purple and pink sunset paint itself across the distant mountains, I feel safe . . . and full of joy.

Old childhood home

My maternal grandfather

The Magic of Creativity

Trigger Warning: Medium

The Beginning of My Creative Journey

I used to think of myself as boring. My closet contained only muted colors. I hid my figure in baggy, shapeless clothes. I was studious, ultra-reliable, and extremely helpful but, by my own assessment, not particularly interesting. How did I evolve into an independent filmmaker whose personal documentaries have been viewed by several hundred thousand people?

It all started when I took a creativity class. The class was offered at a community college and cost just $99. It did not seem like a big deal at the time. But it changed my life!

The class was my attempt to do something just for fun. It would be just for me, some "mom time."

My older son was headed to middle school in a year. This would be my last year as his homeroom mom. I had been homeroom mom every year that my sons were in elementary school, which can be considered a status symbol for an elementary school student but not so for a mature middle schooler.

One day, instead of going to my sons' elementary school as usual, I drove to the local community college. Creativity was an "adult education" class. There were twenty-one students, all women. We sat in wooden desks designed for college students. I had forgotten how uncomfortable they were, especially for my forty-year-old body! None of us could be mistaken for college coeds. I was not the only one shifting in my chair.

We introduced ourselves by telling our reason for taking the class. The answers given included to become a professional chef, to direct films, to make use of the art degree she got when she was *much* younger, to design clothes, to paint a mural, and, from at least five people, to write a novel. My answer: "I'm taking this class for my own enjoyment. That's the only reason."

Our "textbook" was *The Artist's Way: A Spiritual Path to Higher Creativity* by Julia Cameron. The premise of the book is that to create, you need to feel treasured, like an extremely well-cared for child. The book and the teacher exhorted each of us to provide this level of nurturing to ourselves. As an adult, the only person from whom I can receive complete comfort is me.

Cameron spent her early adult life as a successful screenplay writer and as an alcoholic. When she quit drinking, she quit writing. She found her way back to creativity through self-care. She preaches the importance of daily journaling. This journaling needs to be done first thing in the morning, before your feet hit the floor. I found that by religiously doing "morning pages," I often could remember my dreams.

Another essential part of Cameron's creativity campaign is to take yourself on something that she calls an "artist date." It is taking yourself on an outing that your younger self would have enjoyed. Examples include visiting an art museum, taking a finger-painting class, browsing at a bookstore, window shopping at an exclusive boutique, and going on a carnival ride. It should be just for fun and just you, a solo outing (although I do cheat sometimes and bring another art lover along).

The class took place every Wednesday evening for thirteen weeks. By week eight, the original twenty-one students had dwindled down to five. By week ten, there were only three of us. The three of us kept in touch for a while after the class ended. To my knowledge, I alone remain involved in creative endeavors.

Why do so many people quit before finishing their artistic projects? Creativity is hard work! It can be exhausting to care for a newborn, and the same is true of nurturing your fledgling artist self. But, if you provide the right conditions, creativity can expand until it feeds your soul.

By the end of the creativity class, I wanted to write a short story. However, I was told that the novel-writing class at this community college was better than the one focusing on short stories, so I took it. I loved the teacher. The next semester, I took her advanced class. It was for screenplay writers as well as for aspiring novelists. I met a student in that class who liked an idea that I had for a novel and offered to cowrite if we could use the idea for a screenplay before writing the novel. He quit as my cowriter before we finished the script, but I was already hooked. Screenplay writing, with its strict page count expectations, is like poetry. It depends heavily on symbolic images. The focus is "show, don't tell." I began to visualize what I wanted my viewers to see on screen. I learned to delete all unnecessary dialogue.

Sister Mary's Angel

··

Sister Mary's Angel, PG-13, is a romantic comedy with depth. It is my fun film. Runtime is eighty-seven minutes. It stars identical twins Kris and Alix Angelis. It is available to view free of charge on my website and on my YouTube channel.

··

The screenplay that I wrote was *Sister Mary's Angel*, a fictional story about identical twin sisters. Angel, a lingerie model, has an urgent need for medical care. She has no savings, no health insurance, and no options in her pre-Obamacare world. She trades places with her identical sister, a nun, so that the Catholic Church will pay for her surgery. It is a dramatic comedy with child abuse in the backstory.

The idea for *Sister Mary's Angel* came to me when I was at Starbucks with an elderly, vivacious ex-nun from my book club. She said, "When I became a nun, there were two paths for a Catholic girl who had been molested: become a nun or become a prostitute." In my original draft, the lingerie model was a prostitute. (Back then, I used the term "prostitute" rather than "sex trafficking victim" which is the term that I always use now.) I changed the character based on advice from Jean Smart. I saw her when we both were in the audience at a film conference. I recognized her from her iconic role in the sitcom *Designing Woman* from the 1980s and 1990s. I rushed up to her, not knowing what to say except for the elevator pitch for my script. Smart told me that my script would be more appealing to someone like her if its characters were more subtle.

I was passionate about the script because it contains a sermon. The convent priest knows that the sisters switched places, but he does not report them. Having been told about the switch in confession, he is bound to confidentiality. The lingerie model, although not Catholic, comes to trust him during her time in the convent. She asks him, "Where was God when my dad used to mess with me?" The kind priest answers, "Angel, I can't know the answer to that for you, but for me, when my dad used to beat me, God was there. He was holding my hand, and He was crying." The words of the priest came from my own personal experience, and I cherish the opportunity to share them with fellow survivors through film.

I made many attempts to sell this script. I got good at pitching it, but then again, I had lots of practice! I went to the Austin (Texas) Film Festival and to the Willamette Writers Conference (Portland, Oregon) multiple times. There I met agents and producers. My script went to Hollywood by invitation, but my eventual reply was always a "No" (often the Hollywood "No," which means that I never heard back).

After a decade of fruitless effort, I decided that if I shot a couple of scenes of the movie, I would have an easier time selling the script. In 2006, I took my first filmmaking class. I thought that was all that I would need to do. I later found that far more effort and resources were needed.

In my filmmaking class, my teacher asked us to make a short, relatively simple film. It had to be less complicated than any of the scenes in my script for *Sister Mary's Angel*. The film that I produced was titled *One Man's Anger, One Woman's Love*. It is described in the next section of this essay.

After I had successfully made a short film, I naively thought I was sufficiently knowledgeable to make a long one. If I had known enough to correctly estimate the time and money that making a narrative fictional film requires, I never would have made one.

My first attempt to make *Sister Mary's Angel* was during the summer of 2009. As I look back, I wonder how I had the gumption to spend my time and money on filmmaking when I was living in a shared house and could barely pay rent. I badly underestimated the cost. On the other hand, I experienced success as I made cold calls to find free filming locations. I not only got permission to film in the Portland Rose Festival carnival area, but I also was granted media passes so that we could enter without paying the admission fee.

Experienced local actors volunteered to play the supporting roles, but I needed identical twins to be the stars. I found a set of twins on Craigslist who lived 100 miles away. They had hardly any acting experience and yet turned out to be prima donnas. I offered them no financial reimbursement, but, since I was filming on a weekend when the other people in my shared house would be out of town, I agreed to let them sleep in our living room. Instead, they insisted on sleeping in a bedroom that I had no right to use. I allowed them to use the bedroom and, as a result, was kicked out of the house. This experience showed me that I probably never would be able to produce my film. However, soon after, there was a major change in my personal life.

I met my husband Jerry while I was in the midst of working on the film. Four months after we started dating, Jerry's ninety-five-year-old mother died, and he received an inheritance. Jerry wanted to contribute a large portion to charity, but I convinced him that my film would be a great way to help people. Before we were even engaged, Jerry agreed to cover my new $15,000 budget, which ultimately turned into an expenditure of well over $50,000. When people turn to me for advice on how to fund a film, I tell them that I have none.

The twins who appeared in the film were not the ones

whom I originally had selected. I found out that I qualified for the SAG (Screen Actors Guild) Ultra Low Budget category, which enabled me to pay union actors a flat fee of $100 a day. I found actors on the SAG website who listed "twins" under special abilities. However, I found that some had a twin sibling, but the sibling was not an actor, or they both acted but were not identical. Finally, I found identical twins, Kris and Alix Angelis.

Kris lived in Seattle and offered to drive to Portland for an audition. Rather than purchase an airline ticket for Alix, I asked Kris to audition for both of them. She was great! Kris told me that her sister Alix is a better actor than her, which is something Alix would never say. Almost all the people who view the film think the twins are equally talented, but every now and then, someone will express a preference. What is interesting is that when they do, half say Alix, and the other half say Kris.

The 2012 Willamette Writers Conference was an easy drive from my Portland, Oregon, suburb. I knew that Hollywood agents, managers, and producers arrive at the hotel the day before the conference. I saw film executive Luke Ryan, who had a first-look deal with Tri-Star at the time. He was waiting in line to check in. He remembered me from previous conferences. (Most people do after hearing about my extreme childhood abuse.) I told him that I had finished editing a couple of scenes for my film and asked him to watch for three minutes. His look said to me that he wished he could get out of it but he did not know how to do so. Ryan sat beside me, watching the clip on my laptop. When he got back to Los Angeles, he watched the full eighty-seven-minute film and showed it to his business partner. Sadly, they ultimately rejected it.

I never was able to sell *Sister Mary's Angel.* I still am glad that I made it. I joke with Jerry that, someday, when we are in an old folk's home, we will have fun watching it. We will brag about it to the other elderly residents. You do not have to wait for the nursing home showing! You can view it on my website and my YouTube channel.

I think of this film as though it were my daughter. Parental pride compels me to include the Willamette Week review. This local paper announced *Sister Mary's Angel*'s 2014 Portland, Oregon, premiere. Its reviewer gave the film four stars out of five, more stars than it did the Meryl Streep movie that came out the same week!

Sister Mary's Angel premiere at Joy Theatre

REVIEW OF SISTER MARY'S ANGEL
BY WILLAMETTE WEEK

Local filmmaker Mary Knight was a social worker for 23 years and later earned recognition for *One Man's Anger, One Woman's Love*, a semi-autobiographical film exploring verbal domestic abuse. So, at first glance, it seems a bit strange for her to follow that film with *Sister Mary's Angel*, a risqué chronicle of two estranged twins—one a nun, the other a lingerie model—trading places. The swap occurs after the penniless lingerie model, Angel, is diagnosed with breast cancer and the nun, Mary, hatches a plan so Angel can tap into the church's generous medical coverage. The film is downright satirical, complete with a nosy senior nun, an altruistic suitor vying for innocent Mary's affection and a freshly nunnified Angel stripping off her habit on a public bus. But as it progresses, Knight's focus on abuse resurfaces, introducing dark themes that contrast with the otherwise whimsical tone. . . . *Sister Mary's Angel* is, above all, a story of rekindled sisterhood and a triumph over both sexual repression and objectification.

If you are not a filmmaker, you may be wondering how I managed to spend more than $50,000. That is a lot of money! If you are a filmmaker, you are wondering how I made any kind of film on so little money. I underpaid every single person who worked for me. Each time I see the film, I appreciate the efforts of all the volunteers and underpaid individuals who made *Sister Mary's Angel* possible! It was a labor of love for everyone who worked on it.

We shot *Sister Mary's Angel* in twenty-two days. The timing worked for us to again use the carnival area of the annual Portland Rose Festival. I needed additional locations. My first indoor location was secured when I gathered the courage to walk up to the register at Portland's iconic Movie Madness video store, and the owner just happened to be present. Three Doors Down, an upscale restaurant, donated space, charging only the cost of one employee's hourly wage.

Jerry and I got married at the church where the wedding scene was shot

A medical doctor let us use his office early in the morning before he opened for business, and his reception-ist was so excited about being on a film set that she volunteered to be there. I appreciated what they did so much that I transferred to them for ongoing medical care. The wedding scene took place at the church I attended, and for the funeral, we used a wedding chapel that was originally a church building. We needed to build a set for the lingerie model's apartment, where much of the film was shot. I persuaded Jerry to let me use his office. I thought his office would be completely functional while being used as a set, but I was wrong. With a king-size bed donated from a local mattress store and walls painted by a highly creative, budget-oriented volunteer art director, it looked so much like a lingerie model's apartment that the longtime UPS delivery person came in the door one day and then left thinking he had come to the wrong place.

My husband Jerry and almost everyone else who had any part in making the film is an extra in it. If you look closely, you can see Jerry's brief appearance in the first scene. I am in the first bus scene, clad in wacky Mickey Mouse overalls. You might not recognize me, as my hair was dyed reddish brown back then. I am in the bus seat behind Alix Angelis, who plays the lingerie model character named Angel. Since her character is posing as a nun and is dressed in a full-length nun habit, a Catholic woman approaches her to ask for marital advice. Angel/Alix tries to help the woman and, in a not so nun-like manner, inquires about her sex life. On camera, you can see my shocked expression peek through as Alix asks the alarmed, modestly dressed, ultra-pious Catholic character, "Is he good in bed?"

Most makers of independent low-budget films do not request a rating from the Motion Picture Association because of the cost. I consider the $3,000 that I paid to get *Sister Mary's Angel* rated well worth the cost. The fee charged is on a sliding scale based on the film budget. I paid the minimum. Steven Spielberg invests over $20,000 per film for the exact same service that I received. *Sister Mary's Angel* was given a PG-13 rating, which is what I wanted. I was surprised to receive a phone call from a member of the rating committee. My smile wide, I cradled the phone as I was told that they were impressed with the film's message.

One Man's Anger, One Woman's Love

....

One Man's Anger, One Woman's Love, *runtime fifteen minutes, is a film about verbal abuse in marriage. It is on my YouTube channel and includes Spanish subtitles. Domestic violence organizations that want a free download to use for educational purposes can contact me through my website, www.MaryKnightProductions.com*

....

I was raw from my 2003 divorce, and the film that I made in my first filmmaking class evolved from that experience. It did not start out as a script, but rather as a private letter to my sons. Sitting on the floor of my third-floor walk-up apartment sobbing, I tried to think of a way to explain to my sons that I wanted them to emulate their father's good traits but to be completely unlike him in the way that he treated me. I was a victim of extreme verbal abuse. That tear-stained letter became a script. My teacher insisted that it needed to be simplified, so the main character in the script has only one son.

I later replaced the film school version of *One Man's Anger, One Woman's Love* with a higher quality fifteen-minute film. It has an uplifting ending that shows that the domestic violence cycle can break. I left my first marriage one month after my older son graduated from high school. Just before leaving home for college, he saw me stand up for myself. My son, unlike his father, is a good husband.

Shortly before my January 2013 premiere of *One Man's Anger, One Woman's Love,* I had a chance encounter with newscaster Reggie Aqui (who, incidentally, recently was named one of *People* magazine's hottest anchors). He liked the film's message and, with one stipulation, wanted to interview me for his Portland, Oregon, network news program. The stipulation was that I must state publicly that the film is about me. I originally had planned to hide my identity and that of the others in the film for the sake of my grown sons' privacy. At the same time, I wanted to help my fellow survivors by getting word out about it. I thought about asking permission from my sons, but I decided not to. My sons knew there had been a time when I would go back into the house to change clothes because their father, my first husband, did not like what I was wearing to church. I was no longer that person. I called each of my sons and informed them that I would be going public. Neither complained.

On a clear January day, Reggie Aqui arrived at our home with a cameraperson. I had been married to Jerry for three years. I asked him to show his support by sitting in the adjacent room while Aqui interviewed me. My awareness that Jerry cherishes me served as my magical armor while I described the abuse that I experienced in my first marriage. On camera, in answer to a question, I told Aqui that my parents used me in child pornography. When the segment aired on television the next day, I went public not only about the verbal abuse in my first marriage but also about being sex trafficked by my parents.

As a result of my news interview, I received the 2013 Triumph Award from Clackamas Women's Services, an Oregon-based nonprofit. As a part of accepting the award, I was asked to speak at their gala banquet fundraising event. The organizers decided that a short film clip could be useful in soliciting contributions. Because I was a filmmaker, they hired me to make a five-minute film about myself! I have been hired as a filmmaker on only a few occasions, and this was definitely the most interesting time. I hired a camera person to take footage of my speech at the Gala Banquet without knowing how I would use it. In my speech, wearing the only evening gown that I ever have purchased, I said, "When I was a little girl, my perpetrators said terrible things would happen if I ever told what they did to me. I told, and I'm getting this awesome award in front of a room full of people!" That footage appears at the end of my film *Am I Crazy? My Journey to Determine if My Memories Are True.*

One Man's Anger, One Woman's Love has been shown to domestic violence survivors worldwide. I found out first-hand that its message can travel across cultures. When it was screened at the Oregon World Affairs Council to representatives from twelve Arab nations, I saw tears fall. I am glad that I decided to go public about the verbal abuse I experienced in my first marriage.

Personal Documentaries and Essays

During the summer of 2013, I started preparations for two major projects. The stories of how these projects were completed are intertwined. Both involved disappointment in the early stages but ended in success.

In June and July, I took an eight-week documentary class at Northwest Film Center in Portland with the goal of making a personal documentary about my recovery from childhood abuse. I was told that a documentary is interesting only when something actually happens on camera. The teacher did not like the idea of a film about past abuse, as it only could be shown in retrospect. I was discouraged. My film class ended, and during the entire month of August 2013, I worked on an application for the master of fine arts' creative nonfiction program at Pacific University in Forest Grove, Oregon. I wanted to become a better writer to help me complete this memoir.

There were three requirements for admission: a literary critical analysis (I had to use Google to find out what those words meant!), a personal essay, and a writing sample. I had not taken an English class since high school. I worked hard and begged for help from my friends and acquaintances, including a farmer with a master's degree in English. Pacific University was impressed enough with my literary critical analysis essay and my personal essay to give me a second chance on my writing sample. My writing sample was filled with examples of horrendous childhood abuse, which a Pacific University staff member described as "no more than a listing of events." I was told that it was rare to be given a second chance and advised to focus on a single incident. I wrote an essay that has since evolved into "My Parents Were KKK Members and Pedophiles." It is about the murder of a Black family that I witnessed when I was eight years old. Subsequently, I received some confusing communication from the university. I received an acceptance letter the day after I had received an email explaining that I could not be accepted unless I included "facts" such as "the names of victims" and "quotes from the newspaper or obituaries." Otherwise, my essay could be accepted only as fiction, not as creative nonfiction.

I sat at my dining table digesting the email, instructing my body to take one breath and then another. After twenty or so breaths, I picked up my phone. My hands trembled as I dialed the number of the administrator who sent me the email. Willing my voice to stay steady, I explained, to no avail, why I had none of the requested information. Tears splashed the tabletop as I put down the phone. I doubted myself in a way that I had not since the early 1990s when I first remembered my child abuse. "If I really believe all this is true, why haven't I hired a private investigator? Is it because deep down I don't believe it?" I grabbed my phone and called my husband Jerry at his office. I told him that I want us to hire a private investigator. Jerry immediately agreed to help me.

A couple of nights later, in our small apartment bedroom, as we were about to go to sleep, Jerry said, "I think this could cost a lot. Maybe $50,000 or more. That's fine with me, but I don't want you to complain about spending the money." I know that my husband does not start something that he does not plan to see through to the very end. I was sure that I would rather spend $50,000 on filmmaking than on an investigation, especially since finding evidence of crime that took place in 1963 is unlikely.

I woke up the next morning with the title for my documentary, *Am I Crazy?* Exploring the question of whether something is true or not works well in documentaries. I premiered the finished film, *Am I Crazy? My Journey to Determine if My Memories Are True*, in 2017. In 2022, the film was revised, and new scenes were added. I tell more about the process of making it later in this essay. The success of my film overshadowed the rejection that gave it birth.

In writing this essay, I was reminded of the profound effect that being denied admittance by Pacific University had on me. I had lost all confidence in myself as a creative nonfiction writer. I felt that I had no choice but to hire a writing coach when, during the Black Lives Matter summer of 2020, I had an urgent, overwhelming compulsion to publicly disclose the KKK atrocity that I witnessed. I hired a writing coach who was supportive emotionally, but her suggestions for changes to my wording were minimal. That was when I decided to write my memoir by myself.

I now know that, since my essay submission to Pacific University was written from the perspective of my child self, it need only contain the information available to me at age eight. I wonder if my essay would be acceptable to

Pacific University today. Survivors now are treated much differently than we were in 2013, thanks to Dylan Farrow and the other champions of the #MeToo movement.

Pacific University had rejected my essay partly because it did not contain "the names of the victims," as though being made to witness murder as a child is not a traumatic event. I had a palpable fear about how Black individuals would react to my essay. I thought they would be angry at me for the actions of my parents. That has not been my experience.

I always ask several people to read and comment on my writing before I publish it. This time, I made a commitment to have at least as many Black as white beta readers. I looked through my Facebook friends, and almost all the faces were white. I felt ashamed of myself. I had not been aware of my level of racial insulation, or should I say, suffocation. After attending a conference with Armand King, author of *Raised in Pimp City: The Uncut Truth About Domestic Sex Trafficking*, I stayed in touch with him. King is Black. I asked him, "Is the story I am telling so offensive it should be left untold?" He replied that I definitely should publish it.

In my Toastmasters club, one of our best speakers was Kory Thomas May, who also is Black. His touching feedback to my essay was "You are illuminating a path to healing. Your story must be told, as this is not your burden to carry." Through May's Facebook page, I met another fellow Toastmaster from across the country: Barbara Beckley, also Black. She gave me such a helpful critique that I hired her as a consultant for my website. Later, I was her guest on *The Diamond Factor* podcast.

I found the rest of the Black beta readers by friending friends of my new Facebook friends. My world expanded, and my essay benefitted from the feedback. For example, I quit capitalizing the word white when referring to a person and left out an unnecessary detail that could have been misinterpreted.

I was interviewed about the essay by a dozen podcast hosts, most of whom were Black. My first interview was by Aaron Devon King, a talented Black actor and podcaster. King's wife gave birth to their first child, a little girl, only three weeks prior to our recording session. I always will remember King's tenderness toward me and the sound of his gasp when I described what my father had done. One of my pandemic blessings has been to watch King's daughter grow up via Facebook postings.

Dr. Vanessa Dunn Guyton and her mother Geneva Dunn on my back porch with me. I was thrilled that I finally got to meet them in person!

I am the only white member of a weekly art therapy group facilitated by Dr. Vanessa Dunn Guyton, another podcast host who interviewed me about my KKK experience. At a recent meeting, a member in her thirties, who is the member most likely to bring laughter to our group, instead told us that her fifteen-year-old niece was missing. She prefaced her comment by saying, "I'm sorry, Mary, but I have to say . . ." Then she told about the lack of media attention for her relative, which was a sharp contrast from the many newspaper articles about a white teen who had been reported missing at about the same time. I felt guilty about having nothing to offer other than a post on my Facebook page. (That offer was readily accepted).

I feel like I had more life-altering experiences during the pandemic than I would have had if I had traveled across the world. I always will treasure the virtual friendships that resulted from my writing the KKK essay.

Am I Crazy? My Journey to Determine if My Memories Are True

. . . .

My personal documentary, Am I Crazy? My Journey to Determine if My Memories Are True *(2022), runtime 103 minutes, is about my own recovered memories of extreme childhood abuse. It is on my YouTube channel and can also be viewed on my website under the "Films" tab. It is available with Spanish, German, and French subtitles, as well as with English closed caption. www.MaryKnightProductions.com*

. . . .

On the October 2013 morning when I woke up with a title in mind for this documentary, I had no idea the film would end up being watched by so many people. I just knew I needed to reevaluate the memories that surfaced for me in 1993. My parents were deceased, so they could not be interviewed. Instead, I interviewed people who reminded me of them. A year before I remembered my abuse, an organization was founded to aid accused parents. It was called the

False Memory Syndrome Foundation (FMSF). My parents were members. I interviewed the cofounder of FMSF and two of its board members for my documentary. I tell more about this organization and go into detail about these interviews in my essay "My Encounters with the False Memory Syndrome Foundation."

In making this film, I also interviewed three people that I consider to be heroes: former Miss American Marilyn Van Derbur and psychiatrists Dr. Bessel Van der Kolk and Dr. Susie Weit. Marilyn Van Derbur is my hero because of her extensive survivor advocacy work. She was crowned Miss America in 1957. Four years later, her memories of paternal incest came flooding back into her conscious mind. She had repressed all memory of this abuse until that time. She did not speak publicly about it until 1991. Hers was the cover story in *People* magazine in June of that year. I learned of her story from an unlikely source: my mother. I was in full contact with my parents until I remembered my abuse in 1993. During a visit in the summer of 1991, my mother and I were up late one night talking. Although I had not remembered my own abuse, my mother knew that I was counseling survivors of child sexual abuse. With the animated demeanor she used when discussing celebrities, my mother told me about Marilyn Van Derbur and wondered aloud why anyone would disbelieve a credible person who had no reason to seek attention by reporting something that is not true. My mother even gave me her copy of the *People* magazine that had Marilyn on the cover. In about 1994, after watching a video of a presentation by Marilyn, I confronted my mother about not believing my reports of abuse. My mother did not dispute that I also am a credible person who had no reason to seek attention by reporting something that is not true. Her only comment was, "Yes. It is odd."

FMSF discounts all survivors who report recovered memories of child abuse. Van Derbur's account is especially problematic for them because she is well known. I asked each of the FMSF proponents I interviewed about Van Derbur. I include some of their responses in my film and in the essay "My Encounters with the False Memory Syndrome Foundation." Interviewing people who did not know Van Derbur and yet were willing to say negative things about her had been the hard part. I wanted to talk directly to Van Derbur. I was thrilled when she agreed to a telephone interview. I had an old flip phone at the time, but my cinematographer let me use her iPhone. I fumbled with it, too nervous about the interview to figure out how to operate unfamiliar technology. When I finally was able to make the call, Marilyn answered. I savored the sound of her voice. I told her about the day that I sat on the sofa watching her video presentation on my television. In it, Marilyn said to her live audience, "If you're a survivor and you are comfortable standing, you may do so now." Alone in my living room, I stood up. In that moment, I knew that I wanted to do for ritual abuse survivors what Marilyn was doing for incest survivors. When I told Van Derbur about this goal, she said, "And that's what you're doing." That was when I realized that making *Am I Crazy? My Journey* was fulfilling the most important item on my bucket list.

Van Derbur asked me if I had considered interviewing "Bessel." She was referring to Dr. Bessel Van der Kolk, author of *The New York Times*'s "Science" bestseller *The Body Keeps the Score.* Van der Kolk is a neuroscientist, researcher, and psychiatrist. I purchased his book. I knew from page 1 that I wanted to interview him. He did not become my hero, however, until I read chapter 16, in which he extolls the healing power of yoga, which is a passion of mine.

When Van der Kolk agreed to be in my film, I was so excited that I could not sleep for two nights. I knew his involvement would attract additional viewers, and it has. Van der Kolk agreed to give me an hour of his time immediately after finishing a two-day seminar in Portland, Oregon, which is where I was living. His on-camera explanation of traumatic memory is easily understood. When viewers contact me about my film, they often quote from the Van der Kolk interview.

I had not heard of child/adolescent psychiatrist Dr. Susie Weit before meeting her. I had traveled to a child abuse conference in Salt Lake City to interview two people, neither of whom appeared in my documentary because of a disagreement over what details needed to be included. I met Dr. Weit on the first day of the conference and was impressed by her passion for helping abuse survivors. I already had arranged to fly a cinematographer in for a one-day film shoot. Weit rearranged her schedule for that day to give me thirty minutes. It was the easiest interview that I had ever done. Weit was not only knowledgeable, she was also compassionate. My feelings had been hurt by other professionals at the conference who treated me like I was a filmmaker making a documentary about a child abuse survivor, rather than a survivor making a personal documentary. Weit listened to my account of childhood abuse with tender empathy. She became my hero that day. Weit's knowledge base is much the same as that of Van der Kolk.

Is Filmmaking Therapeutic?

People question me if my filmmaking is therapeutic. I used to cringe when asked this question, as though it was a way of minimizing me as a person, not to mention as an artist.

Now I proudly say that my films are therapeutic, both for me and for my viewers.

While filming *Am I Crazy? My Journey to Determine if My Memories Are True*, I came to a place of acceptance related to my abusive father. I made two trips to his grave in that film, and it is obvious on camera that my attitude toward him changed between those visits. On the other hand, each time that I viewed the film after completing it, my gut reminded me that I had additional emotional work to do related to my mother. On Mother's Day weekend in 2019, I dragged myself to my mother's grave. I have not visited it since. I hired a photographer to document the visit. I screamed at her until my throat stung, and I felt righteous doing so. I pounded my fist on her gravestone so hard it hurt. I sobbed until I came to my own rescue. I am glad that I have a recording of the commitment that I made to myself to be, from that day forward, my own mother. That footage is in my documentary *Mothers and Molestation: A Film about Child Abuse*, which premiered at the 2022 Virtual Global Summit to End Sexual Exploitation.

A testimony to the therapeutic effect filmmaking had on me came during a recent phone call with Bradley Sellers, the primary cinematographer for *Am I Crazy? My Journey*. His credentials are impressive. He was director of photography for the first season of the television show *Curb Your Enthusiasm*. Afterward, he left Los Angeles because he and his wife did not consider it the best place to raise their young children. They moved to Portland, Oregon, which is where I lived. Sellers is highly skilled. I am grateful that he agreed to work on this film for a fraction of his usual fees. He worked a ten-hour day when we flew roundtrip to Irvine, California, for an interview with FMSF Board Member Dr. Elizabeth Loftus. This was a difficult interview for me. With contained frustration, I listened as Loftus discounted former Miss America Marilyn Van Derbur's recollections. Loftus said, "I've read a whole lot more than just *People* magazine about that case." Later in the interview, Loftus contradicted her initial statement by admitting that her only information about Van Derbur was "newspaper knowledge." Loftus used the words "your claims" when referring to my disclosures of childhood sexual abuse. She stated that there is no "credible evidence" of recovered memories. While waiting for our late-night flight home, I tried to talk to Sellers about my interactions with Loftus. He made a comment that caused me to wonder if he agreed with some of the statements Loftus made. I was exhausted and, rather than pursue our conversation, chose not to sit by him on the plane. I worked with Sellers again after that and was able to convince myself that I had misunderstood what he said during our day trip to California.

In preparation for writing this essay, I called Sellers and asked him to tell me his thoughts on the Loftus interview. He said that Loftus had articulated some valid points. I told him that I have gotten comments from multiple survivors who say, "When I heard what Loftus said, I wished I could jump into the screen and strangle her." Sellers said, "That must be because of the way you edited it." As I thought about how to reply, I noticed how calm I was. This was a conversation I had been putting off for years. Standing outside, I was aware of fresh air coming into my lungs. I told Sellers that no one could edit that footage in a way that survivors would be comfortable with Loftus's statements. I ended the phone call with a pleasant exchange. I had *Curb Your Enthusiasm* questions since I had watched the program for the first time only recently. Sellers answered my questions. (Yes, Larry David really is a nice guy.) I asked him about his family, and he asked me about my husband. Sellers is a nice person and a good family man. While making my film, I developed the sense of self that is necessary when people must agree to disagree.

On the last day of filming *Mothers and Molestation*, I practiced self-care in a way that I had never done before. I knew the crew would be supportive of me since I had hired them previously. Still, I made arrangements for Production Assistant Haley Baker to be present throughout the day. The only payment Baker wanted was film credit since acting is her hobby. Her day job is behavior modification specialist. Her qualifications for that role are a master's degree in psychology and the capacity for deep empathy. *Mothers and Molestation* is narrated through information that I share in a lecture format. All morning, I stood and lectured to an audience consisting of actors. By midmorning I became faint and craved a chance to sit down and rest. I kept going so that the audience members could go home at noon as scheduled. At lunch when Baker was making sandwiches for the crew, I drank a whole bottle of water. Then I found a quiet, isolated hallway outside of the women's restroom. I was wearing leggings. I decided to put my legs up the wall in a relaxing yoga pose. After clearing my mind for fifteen minutes, I went back to the impromptu snack area. While she handed me the peanut butter and jelly sandwich she made for me, Baker and I sat and discussed the morning shoot from an emotional, rather than a filmmaking, perspective. If you are considering telling your story through film, I advise you to have a support person on set at all times. Everyone needs a Haley Baker! This is a role I might consider filling for a fellow survivor/aspiring documentarian.

My Current Creative Endeavors

I am an extrovert, which works well for me as a filmmaker.

I love collaboration. It is fun to be in the same room with people who are more talented than me. Gathering those people on a low budget requires a huge amount of creativity. And yet, I will not shoot another full-length film. Feature-length filmmaking is simply too expensive. Jerry and I gave a high financial priority to filmmaking. I appreciate my husband for many reasons, including that he has made it possible for me to be a full-time artist (and survivor activist). Feature films take years to complete. Short films can be finished in a matter of days, weeks, or months. I will continue to edit short films, either from the footage I have already taken or from recordings I make of future Zoom interviews. Some of these films will focus on fellow child abuse survivors instead of on me.

Unlike filmmaking, writing does not cost a lot of money. Sometimes it has seemed too expensive for me emotionally, though. It is an individual endeavor that can make me shiver with aloneness. As a child, whenever possible, I tucked myself away from my abusive family, bedroom door firmly closed. I felt lonely, even as I allowed myself to pretend to be safe from harm. Inside my adult world, in total safety, I sometimes ache from loneliness while composing my thoughts and writing them down. I wondered if I should quit writing after finishing my memoir. Then, while driving one rainy night, I listened to a CD by Elizabeth Gilbert. She became famous for *Eat, Pray, Love,* but this book was *Big Magic.* It is about the creative process. Gilbert despises the myth that all artists must suffer, saying it is completely untrue. Creativity should be an expression of joy. I could not imagine joy outshining my feeling of isolation until Gilbert told about the impact she had on bestselling author Brene Brown, who always had dreaded the writing process. Brown invited two friends to an all-expenses-paid beachhouse weekend. The weekend retreat was Gilbert's idea.

The three women sat in the living room. Her friends held notepads and took notes, while Brown, empty-handed, told stories related to her subject matter. Then she went into another room and typed the notes. When she came back and read the notes aloud, her friends asked questions to help her clarify her thoughts.

This seemed like an amazing process, but not one that I can afford. At around the same time, I discovered a free online group called Corporeal Writing. In this group, unlike the writing groups that I had been in before, we spend most of our meeting time actively writing. Participants from all over the nation meet for two hours on Mondays and Fridays. At the end of the session, we read what we have written aloud. I look forward to these sessions and find in them a source of encouragement for happy writing even when I am alone.

My creativity is not limited to writing and producing short films. It is much broader than that, and it has run a full circle. Creativity connects me with the parts of myself that I held dear before ever considering that I could be artistic. I started baking while in grade school, following the cookbook to the letter. Now I feel adventuresome as I toss together an untried combination of vegetables into a cooking pot or add a unique ingredient while baking. Some of my favorite creative moments were figuring out how to entertain and discipline my pre-school sons. As I age, my wardrobe is getting a bit boring again, but inside, I am a neon gazelle.

I make up my own recipe for being a supportive, fun grandma and foster parent. One day, snuggled away in my bedroom with my laptop, I was called away mid-sentence by a hungry twelve-year-old. I made my way to the kitchen while my mind recited the promise that I had made to myself of a day focused on artistic endeavors. Standing at the stove, a spray of hot grease touched my hand. It reminded me that it took lots of creativity for me to discover a well-balanced meal for a young man who insists that he will not eat meat if he sees any fat on it and yet loves bacon.

Creativity, in all its forms, makes my life worth living!

My Encounters with the False Memory Syndrome Foundation

Trigger Warning: Low

In 1997, a columnist for *The Dallas Morning News* replied to a letter from a reader. While looking through her deceased father's possessions, she found his extensive collection of child pornography. She wanted to make a significant financial donation to an organization that helps child abuse survivors, she said, and asked the columnist for a suggestion. Instead of offering a suggestion, the columnist told her to forgive her father. After all, he meant no harm by his actions, the columnist informed her. He went on to say that no one gets hurt in the production of child pornography.

Appalled, I called the columnist. I told him my parents photographed me when I was a little girl, and I listed the many ways I was hurt by it. He said, "Oh, what you are saying can't possibly be true. You have false memories." After he hung up, I was determined to do something to correct the misinformation that he promoted in this column.

Accused parents facing possible lawsuits had joined forces in 1992. They established a nonprofit, the False Memory Syndrome Foundation (FMSF), and invested millions in a public relations campaign to convince society that many child sex abuse allegations are false memories.

The American Psychiatric Association does not recognize a disorder known as "false memory syndrome" and never has. This term is not included in the latest edition of the *Diagnostic and Statistical Manual of Mental Disorders* (*DSM-5-TR*) or in any earlier edition. *DSM-5-TR* is the authoritative guide to the diagnosis of mental disorders. It is used by mental health professionals in the United States and much of the rest of the world.

In response to the *Morning News* column, I also wrote a letter to the editor. The newspaper published my letter along with contact information for Victims of Incest Can Emerge Survivors (VOICES). VOICES was a nonprofit organization that provided therapeutic program facilities and other support for rape and sexual assault survivors. Not long after my response was published, I attended the 1998 VOICES conference. Members of FMSF picketed there. A middle-aged woman carried a sign describing her son as "dead." I asked her what she meant by that. Her reply made it obvious that her son was alive and had started to acknowledge his childhood abuse. This conversation was my first of many with proponents of false memories.

In 2013, I started making my personal documentary, *Am I Crazy? My Journey to Determine if My Memories Are True.* My goal in producing this film at age fifty-seven was to reevaluate the memories that surfaced for me at age thirty-seven. I had believed these memories to be true for twenty years. I thought the best way to truly question myself was to directly question people who, like my deceased parents, say recovered memories are false.

This film has been translated into German, Spanish, and Polish subtitles. (A hypnotherapist in Poland was so impressed he volunteered to translate.) It was first released in 2017 with a run time of 55 minutes. The 2022 version is 103 minutes long. *Am I Crazy? My Journey*, in its various forms—has been viewed by hundreds of thousands of people. It literally has a worldwide following. I am often complimented on this documentary for its objective journalistic truth-telling, and I am proud of it as such. However, that was not my original motivation in making it. There was an unhealed part of me that wanted to believe my memories were false so that I could imagine that my parents were respectable people. Thus, I could be relieved of my long-held guilt. I had been made to watch as my parents tortured other children, some of whom were my childhood friends. Although I was a child at the time, I felt responsible for the actions of my parents. What my parents did was far reaching. If it did really happen, I felt compelled to do something huge to counteract it. Being vulnerable on camera would be my act of contrition.

I often am asked how I had the strength to sit across from proponents of false memories. As I watch my film now, I sometimes wonder the same thing. I will say that I dreaded each of these interviews. I felt physically ill as the interview time approached. I will never do something like that again. I do not suggest other survivors do what I did. Still, I am thankful that I made the film.

My analytical self can point to several factors that aided me in developing the confidence and skills to do these interviews. My choice to go into a helping-people profession was due to my unconscious desire to heal myself. I initially thought that I wanted to do adoption work because my little sister was adopted by my parents. (Yes, that does mean that the adoption social worker who investigated my parents did not discover that they were child molesters.) I kept the real reason for wanting to do adoption work concealed even from myself—guilt derived from witnessing other children being abused.

Doing adoption work requires interview skills. I studiously researched ways to ask questions that would enable me to make sure the prospective adoptive parents were loving. After placing about 100 children in adoptive homes, I had a chance encounter with a psychologist. She was looking for someone to join her practice as a divorce custody evaluator. She convinced me that I had the necessary qualifications.

When judges appointed me to do evaluations in divorce custody cases, I felt respected. I was required to testify in court for some of the cases. The first time I ever felt truly smart was when I was on the witness stand and one of the highest paid attorneys in town made several unsuccessful attempts to discount my evaluation. My court testimony kept improving, as did my confidence. I unknowingly prepared myself for my eventual on-camera conversations with FMSF leaders.

When I thought of the False Memory Syndrome Foundation, Freyd was the name that came to mind. Pamela and her husband Peter created FMSF just eighteen months after their daughter, Dr. Jennifer Freyd, recovered memories of paternal incest. I was surprised that I found Pamela's phone number online. I called it, and she answered. I believe Pamela's reason for agreeing to an interview was that she thought that she could convince me that my memories were false. As I prepared for this interview, it was obvious to me that I had not gotten over the loss of my mother. I decided to bake cookies for Pamela with my mother's recipe.

For two weeks before our February 2014 interview, I had body pain that kept me awake every night. I was questioning my memories of molestation by my mother. I did not want to state publicly (and on camera) that my mother had sexually and physically abused me, so I tried to quit believing that she had. The body pain was accompanied by visual images of horrific abuse by my mother. The pain disappeared each night only after I acknowledged to myself the validity of the memories. Two nights before my interview with Pamela, I decided, in answer to her inevitable question about the identities of my abusers, I would include my mother.

As I arranged for my trip to Philadelphia to interview Pamela Freyd, I hired an entertainment attorney to draft a clearly stated release form that would give me the legal right to use the footage from our interview in my upcoming film. I emailed Pamela the release form. She spent two weeks reviewing it, which gave me the impression she asked her attorney to look at it. Later I remembered that as a filmmaker, I also needed to get a location release signed. I attached this release to an email to Pamela that read, "I need it signed by the owner of the property. I feel bad even asking this because it's none of my business, but, if you don't mind saying, do you rent your home or own it?" Pamela wrote back saying she owned her home.

As it turns out, the Freyd condominium is in one of the most exclusive neighborhoods in Philadelphia. It overlooks Rittenhouse Square Park. I had never been in a building that had a doorman.

I was terrified as I entered Pamela Freyd's building. I thought that she would ask me a question that I had never thought to ask myself, but that didn't happen. I had a huge sense of relief after this interview.

My primary intent was not to ask Pamela personal

questions, but I could not resist attempting to get an answer to the obvious one. Midway through the interview, I asked Pamela why she believed her husband and not her daughter. I did not know whether she would answer. With only slight hesitation, she did answer. Her verbal answer wasn't as interesting as her body language while answering. I hope you will view *Am I Crazy? My Journey to Determine if My Memories Are True* to see this for yourself. Initially, Pamela said that the reason she did not believe her daughter, Dr. Jennifer Freyd, was because Jennifer "refused to talk." There is documentation to the contrary. Jennifer had extensive email communication with her parents after disclosing to them. Later in our interview, a reason Pamela gave for not believing her daughter was that she had known her husband longer than her daughter. Of course!

After my interview with Pamela Freyd, I called FMSF board member and psychologist Dr. Elizabeth Loftus at her University of California Irvine office. I asked to interview her. She said that she did not have time, but she referred me to her fellow FMSF board member Dr. Loren Pankratz, also a psychologist.

Pankratz lives in Portland, Oregon, which is where I was living at the time. He was cordial with me on the telephone and readily agreed to sign releases similar to the ones Pamela Freyd had signed. I interviewed him in March 2014.

When I interviewed Pankratz, I had just spent two months reading nothing except literature written by false-memory proponents. For hours at a time, I sat in my living-room chair, diligently consuming stacks of books by authors associated with FMSF. I refrained from reading literature written by abuse survivors. There were comments in the pro-false-memory books that indicate child abuse, even if it does occur, does not have much impact on the child. I asked Pankratz about this.

Pankratz said, "A child under two really doesn't have memories of anything that happened. So far as we know, children who have been, who've been physically abused, in any way abused, they don't remember that, and it doesn't seem to have any later effect on them."

As Pankratz was making what I know to be an unscientific comment, I remembered the children who I placed for adoption. One baby was diagnosed as failure to thrive. As Pankratz spoke, my arms remembered holding a baby shortly after she came into our care. She did not cuddle toward the warmth of my arms. Instead, she arched her back as though she wanted to get as far from me as possible. I visited the same baby in her adoptive home three months later. She was almost normal in her capacity to receive human touch. Young children are vulnerable and affected by any mistreatment.

My next reaction to Pankratz was anger. How dare he say such things! I knew children were affected by abuse long before I became a social worker. I had this knowledge before age twelve, which is when I first babysat for young children other than my siblings.

My verbal response to him was, "So that's kind of good news for my sons wanting to find babysitters for their kids because their oldest is two, and so even if their kids are beat up a little bit by the babysitter, it's not going to affect them unless there's an injury?"

Pankratz did not reply to my comment. Instead, he said, "And moreover, we know that most abuse of children under two, most real sexual abuse that occurs, has to do with touching, usually not penetration. It's usually not very violent. It's not violent at all. It's usually more curiosity and exploration." That is not true and made no sense to me. I told him that.

Pankratz went on to say, "For example, if a two-year-old

child saw their parents murdered, they wouldn't remember that. That would be a terrible thing to observe for a two-year-old child, but they wouldn't remember it, and therefore wouldn't be affected by it." (Since I am a mental health professional, I feel compelled to explain that most mental health professionals do *not* agree with Pankratz's statements regarding abuse of very young children).

At the time of my interviews with Pamela Freyd and Dr. Pankratz, I thought it was possible that I would quit believing my own recovered memories. I knew that, even if I decided my own memories were not true, I could not be part of an organization that minimizes the effect of child abuse.

I am not sure the exact moment I quit questioning my own memories, but I know it was prior to the time Dr. Elizabeth Loftus decided her schedule had opened up enough to be interviewed by me. When I arranged this interview, I told her that I had questions for her about FMSF, not that I was questioning my memories. When I arrived with two camerapeople, Loftus had forgotten about our appointment. She thought that it was the next day. Yet, she made herself available for the interview. The camerapeople left briefly to get lunch, so they were not there when I handed her a release form to sign. It was at that time that I found out that she thought that I considered the memories I recovered to be false. Before Loftus signed my release form, I explained in no uncertain terms that I recovered memories of extreme abuse that I believe to be true. Loftus is now saying that I "misled" her.

In December of 2021, journalist Phil Fairbanks asked Loftus about her interview that appears in my film *Am I Crazy? My Journey*. Loftus said, "That was awful . . . I don't know why she had this camera on me with this side view the whole time, and, uh, it was very, I felt very sort of misled.

And sorry I cooperated." Fairbanks asked: "Do you feel you were misrepresented?" Loftus replied, "No, just misled." (Fairbanks posted this interview in the blog section of his website on April 24, 2022, philfairbanks.com)

I do not know to what Loftus was referring when she said I had misled her. The footage of our interview makes it clear that I correctly identified myself to her.

I interviewed Loftus for two hours. I was nervous during this interview, not because I thought she would ask me a question that would cause me to doubt my memories, but because of her time constraints compared to my long list of questions. I asked her about several survivors. From my perspective, Loftus seemed to find creative ways to discount every abuse survivor I mentioned.

Dr. Ross Cheit is an attorney and political science professor at Brown University. He is the author of *The Witch-Hunt Narrative: Politics, Psychology, and the Sexual Abuse of Children*, an extensively researched book about child abuse that occurred in day-care centers in the 1980s and 1990s. As an adult, Cheit recovered memories of his own childhood sexual abuse. This abuse was perpetrated by an employee of the choir camp he attended. He used the type of investigative skills one might learn in law school. As a result, he has a tape-recorded confession by his perpetrator. He also found numerous other men who had been sexually abused by the same perpetrator. Some of these men had continuous memories of the abuse, and some had recovered memories. It is impossible to deny that Cheit's childhood abuse has been corroborated.

I asked Loftus about Cheit. She said, "I don't know that he would say he repressed his memory. I mean because he seems to have found corroboration."

Cheit makes it clear that he has a recovered memory. He wrote about his own case in the introduction of his above-mentioned book. He has spoken about it publicly. In 1997, he launched his Recovered Memory Project website. On it, he names 110 people whose recovered memories have been corroborated. Cheit is #23 on this list.

Regarding former Miss America Marilyn Van Derbur's recovered memories, Loftus initially claimed that she had done "extensive research" and knew that the memories were false. As I continued to question her, Loftus admitted she only had "newspaper knowledge" of Van Derbur's life experiences. It seemed to me that Loftus either had not read or did not remember the newspaper articles that had been written about Van Derbur.

People ask me how I felt when I talked to false-memory proponents. Some film viewers note that I looked calm during these interviews. I was not calm. I was nervous at times, but at other times I was enraged. How dare Pamela Freyd discount her own daughter? How dare she lie and say her daughter "refused to talk" when stacks of emails show that was clearly not the case? I was sickened by comments from Pankratz minimizing the impact of the abuse of babies and toddlers. When my questions resulted in Loftus essentially acknowledging she lied when she said that she had researched Marilyn Van Derbur's case, I must admit that I felt a sense of satisfaction.

I also asked Loftus about Laura Pasley. Pasley considers herself a recanter. A recanter is someone who recovered memories of child abuse, and later decides these memories are false. I got Pasley's name and contact information from Pamela Freyd in response to my request to interview a recanter. I interviewed Pasley by telephone. Unlike the uncomfortable feeling I had while interviewing the other false-memory proponents, I felt good while talking to Pasley. She interacted with me without an obvious agenda. She and I told each other about the children in our lives. I pay attention to the value others place on children, and it seemed to me that Pasley cherishes children.

According to Pasley's report, she had a counselor who falsely convinced her that she was a victim of extreme child abuse. She sued him and received a settlement. One of her complaints about her counselor was that he did not seem at all concerned about the sexual abuse she experienced at age nine. This abuse was by a stranger when she was at a public swimming pool. Pasley lost conscious awareness of what happened to her at age nine not long after it happened. Throughout her teenaged years, she did not remember it at all. She described how the memory came back to her at age 25. Here is an excerpt from our conversation:

> **Pasley:** You know, the memory of sexual abuse. I had kind of compartmentalized it. And then one night, we were in a hotel. And I was with my boyfriend at the time. My daughter's father. And it just came flashing back all of a sudden. And I told him (meaning her counselor), but he said it wasn't it. It wasn't deep enough.
>
> **Me:** But that's a recovered memory. If it was compartmentalized, and you didn't remember it.
>
> **Pasley:** It didn't consciously come to mind. I hadn't thought about it in years. But I can tell it actually changed some of my behavior.

By every legitimate definition I know, Laura Pasley had a recovered memory. Yet, she was a poster child for FMSF. Pasley states, "I stepped out on a media tour that was pretty unbelievable for about two and a half years. I gave them (FMSF) all that." Pasley appeared on talk shows and spoke at FMSF conferences. (It should be noted that Pasley continues to be a proponent of false memory and categorizes all recovered memories as false. She considers her memory of abuse at age nine a forgotten memory.)

I talked to Pankratz, Loftus, and Pamela Freyd about the difference between a recovered memory and a forgotten memory. Their explanations did not make sense to me. False-memory proponents deny the validity of all recovered memories, and yet there are some recovered memories that they are either unable or unwilling to label as false. For example, they cannot deny that Dr. Ross Cheit has proof of being sexually assaulted as a child, so they call his memory forgotten. Laura Pasley had been useful to FMSF in the media, and yet she has a noncontinuous memory she considers to be true. Like most survivors of child abuse, Pasley has no external corroboration for this memory. Rather than treating her like other survivors with noncontinuous memories and calling this memory false, they make an exception for her and refer to it as a forgotten memory. A forgotten memory is simply a term used by false-memory proponents for what objectively would be defined as a recovered memory.

In my opinion, FMSF leaders are viscous in their attempts to discount survivors. Their standards for a survivor who is attempting to validate a recovered memory are impossibly high. Their standards for false-memory proponents who discount these recovered memories are nonexistent. An example of this concerns former Miss America, Marilyn Van Derbur. After I asked about her in an interview with Dr. Pankratz, he sent me an email saying that he had corresponded with a woman who went to the University of Colorado with Van Derbur and "knew her well." He went on to discount Van Derbur's recollection and wrote, "There is no outside confirmation, and lots to disconfirm it." Upon request, Dr. Pankratz gave me the telephone number for Eleanor Goldstein. She had gone to the University of Colorado at the same time as Marilyn Van Derbur but, in fact, never knew her personally.

Goldstein said that she took one class that Van Derbur was in. Below is an excerpt from our telephone conversation about her relationship with Van Derbur:

Me: Did you ever sit by each other?

Goldstein: No.

Me: Did you ever meet her father?

Goldstein: No.

Me: Did you ever meet her mother?

Goldstein: No.

Me: Did she ever confide in you?

Goldstein: I'm not saying we knew each other well. We were not buddies.

Me: Would she know your name?

Goldstein: Probably not.

Me: But you knew her. Probably everyone did when she became Miss America.

Goldstein: I didn't pay any attention until years later when she was a supporter of repressed memories.

I emailed Dr. Pankratz again and asked what sources he had other than Eleanor Goldstein. Pankratz admitted that Goldstein was his only source and that he had found out about her from Pamela Freyd. Freyd confirmed to me that she had no source other than Goldstein for information about Marilyn Van Derbur.

When Goldstein first introduced herself to me, she said, "I went to University of Colorado and went to grad school there as well. And then I started a publishing company, which emerged out of my work at the university. We developed a database, which was one of the first databases. We had 60,000 institutions using our services. We were the first to put a database on the Internet. The reason that is important is that that is how I became involved with the issue of memory."

In fact, Goldstein had a personal reason for her interest in "the issue of memory." Her daughter—Dr. Stacy Sharlet, a chiropractor—recovered memories of extreme childhood abuse in the late 1980s. Like almost all FMSF members, Goldstein was desperate to disprove the memories of her adult child.

Sharlet had never gone public and was unsure if she should. Therefore, she did not want me to directly confront her mother about the memories of abuse. (Since that time, Sharlet has decided that she is comfortable discussing her childhood abuse publicly and has talked to me twice on camera.)

My last interview with a false-memory proponent took place in Goldstein's plush Florida home. Our discussion was at times argumentative but, at other times, cordial. My film crew consisted only of my husband. Goldstein served us a nicely arranged cracker and cheese plate midway through the interview. After we had been there two or three hours, I was tired, hungry, and ready to leave. I stood at the door so that I could get footage saying goodbye to Goldstein. I expected a brief, inconsequential exchange. That is not what happened.

Standing beside me at her front door, alternating between

looking at me and facing the camera, Goldstein declared, "We have to help each other and forgive and understand and have empathy and not carry grudges forever and ever. 'He touched me. Oh my God, he touched me. And therefore, he touched me, and he's dead. He's dead.'"

Goldstein told about a time when her sister had been fondled by their uncle. I asked if a family should stay together even if there had been fondling. She punched my arm hard enough that it hurt and told me that the child should say, "Get out of here, Uncle Irving. Leave me alone."

I was stunned. How could anyone expect children to stop an adult from abusing them? A nauseated feeling rose to my throat and stayed there through the end of the next day. Her words were unbelievable. I inquired, "So you think the child should be responsible to do that?"

She said, "Absolutely. I don't think sexual touch is the horror of all horrors. I think we make a big to-do about nothing."

Now, when I think of FMSF, Goldstein's "A big to-do about nothing" comment rings in my ears.

The False Memory Syndrome Foundation closed its doors in 2019. Unfortunately, our society is still affected by its propaganda.

(For well-researched, detailed information about the damage done by FMSF, see Lynn Crook's 2022 book *False Memories: The Deception That Silenced Millions*, www.LynnCrook.com).

True Memories

By Anna Holtzman

Trigger Warning: Low

··

Guest essayist Anna Holtzman is a survivor of childhood sexual trauma. Like me, she recovered memories
of trauma when she was in her thirties. I include this
explanation of her remembering process because of her
simple, easily understood language and logic.

··

At five years old, I loved reciting my favorite nursery rhyme
about an unruly little boy, but I'd always insert my own
name instead of the boy's name. It was an early rebellion
against what I felt to be unfair differences between how
boys and girls were allowed to be. Five-year-old me was a
loud and proud feminist.

As I got older, though, it seemed like a lot of people
dismissed my feelings as wrong. Some insisted that girls
weren't really treated differently—that sexism was a myth.
Others told me that boys and girls *should* be treated differently, because that was the natural order of things. Still

others would say, "That's just the way things are," implying that inequality is unfortunate, but I should just get over it.

I couldn't help wondering: "Am I crazy?"

As I entered my thirties and a career in television, in order to get along socially and professionally, I convinced myself that I really did have all the same opportunities and advantages that men had. We were living in a post-sexist world, and I focused on succeeding in it. There were dynamics at work that felt "off" to me now and then, but I tried to ignore them and push my discomfort away.

Then came a collective feminist reawakening that stopped me in my tracks. For many, it was the outpouring of stories known as #MeToo. For me, it was a similar but slightly earlier wave of online consciousness-raising under the hashtag #YesAllWomen.

Seeing all of these stories about sexism that reflected my own feelings—feelings that I'd pushed away long ago—was a lightbulb moment. I started reading about feminism and about the backlash to feminism that took place during my childhood in the 1980s and early 90s. Suddenly, things started to make sense. I wasn't crazy. I'd just been gaslighted into thinking I was crazy. And now that I could see I wasn't alone, my long-buried childhood emotions came rushing back to me.

Traumatic memory repression and recovery is a lot like this.

How Traumatic Memory Works

Feelings and memories are interwoven parts of our innate survival system—they're integral to how we protect ourselves from danger. When we experience danger, our autonomic nervous system catalogues a variety of data about the danger—such as narrative memory, emotions, sensations, and images—and neural pathways are formed to help us avoid similar danger in the future.

Traumatic memory is essentially fear conditioning. A simple example of fear conditioning looks like this:

At some point in our early lives, we learn that fire is dangerous to touch. We might learn this by touching fire and getting burned, or we might learn this by seeing someone else get burned or by getting scolded or yelled at when we get too close to a flame.

No matter how we learn that fire is dangerous, our learning experience involves a combination of narrative (what happened), emotion (fear) and our senses (sight, sound, smell, touch, taste).

Our nervous system then determines which parts of the experience to file away in order to recognize potential danger and keep us safe in the future. In some cases, the nervous system may determine that it's important to remember the entire narrative of what happened. In other cases, it may determine that the details are unimportant because an emotional association between fire and fear will suffice to keep us safe.

Throughout our lives, we remember that fire is dangerous to touch. Even if we don't remember it consciously or with narrative, we remember it with our emotions and reflexes. We feel afraid of getting burned by fire and we automatically recoil from it. Our feelings about fire are also reflected by the people around us: everyone agrees that fire is dangerous to touch, and this reinforces our conditioning.

Traumatic Memory Repression

Traumatic memory repression happens when there is no available social support for our feelings and memories about a particular danger. When the people we turn to for safety tell us that our emotions and memories are wrong, we repress them in order to protect ourselves from the greater danger of being socially rejected, punished, or shunned. If nobody in our circle is willing to protect us from danger, our nervous system may determine that it's safest to escape reality and pretend the danger isn't happening.

A classic example of this is when a child is sexually abused by their father. Typically, fathers hold a great deal of social capital in the household thanks to patriarchy, adultism (the privileging of adults' rights over those of children), and capitalism (which often makes families financially reliant on the father.)

When the abused child expresses fear or anger toward the father, they are seldom met with support from other family members who depend on the patriarch for survival. Instead of support, the child is often encouraged to bury their feelings and to question their reality. They may even be shunned or punished by family members who seek to secure their own safety by aligning with the patriarch.

Now the child is caught in a dilemma, with two conflicting sets of fear conditioning: On the one hand, their nervous system has learned that Dad's behavior is dangerous. On the other hand, their nervous system has learned that their thoughts and feelings about the abuse are also dangerous.

Children can't survive on their own, so the child's nervous system will usually determine that losing family support would be a much greater danger than Dad's behavior. Accordingly, the neural pathway programmed to remember Dad's dangerous behavior may be overridden and suppressed.

Reawakening

Around the same time that I started rediscovering feminism and validating my feelings about sexism in the workplace, I also started rediscovering another buried trove of memory and emotion that had been bubbling to the surface periodically ever since my first sexual experience as a teen. I never found a safe person to open up to about these feelings in my adolescence, so every time they'd bubble up, I'd shove them way back down until they disappeared for the next few hours, days, months, or even years.

Then in my midthirties, a series of traumatic events rocked my family, and my closet full of unprocessed emotions and memories became too full for me to keep latching the door shut. No longer could I successfully shove everything to the back of my mind and have it stay there. After having been in psychotherapy for five years already, new material started coming up in my sessions that refused to be ignored.

Everyone's experience with memory repression and recovery is different and unique, though many common threads tend to run through them. This is what my experience was like:

It started with memories of memories. I began to fixate on a memory of what I now describe as my first traumatic flashback—though at the time, I had no idea what was happening to me. I was eighteen, and I was sexually experimenting for the first time with a boy my age. It started off the way I expected it to: I felt curious, excited, shy, the beginnings of pleasure . . . and then suddenly something came over me. I felt numb, frozen, disconnected from the world and from my own body.

Looking back now, in my midforties and having become a psychotherapist myself, I'd say that teenage me was dissociating. I remember feeling like everything was going blank, feeling my insides curdle, crumpling into a trembling puddle, and crying inconsolably. I remember feeling frightened, confused, and ashamed. And I remember my mind filling up with thoughts about my parents and the feeling of the way they touched my body, held me close, and kissed me when they were being affectionate. I felt nauseous, sick, and all mixed up. The next morning, I fainted and came to with a raging fever. I still feel emotional now, thinking back to how alone, bewildered, and freaked out I felt then. I remember thinking: "Something's very wrong with me. Maybe I'm crazy."

It's been a slow and gradual journey since that memory came up in therapy in my midthirties. It led to more memories—some were memories of other flashbacks, and some were memories of childhood itself. Some were clear and others very murky. Most were things I'd always remembered but felt too scared or confused to think about for long. Others were little snippets that surfaced once I started allowing myself to talk about those initial memories with my therapist.

As all of these memories began to take up more and more space in my conscious mind, I found myself in constant battle with them. My neural pathways had learned to override my feelings and memories in order to preserve closeness with my parents. Those neural pathways kept sending me messages like

"Your memories aren't real; you made them up."

"Your memories are real, but your feelings are overreactions—these experiences weren't a big deal, it was just a misunderstanding. You're being too sensitive."

"Don't go there—you're just going to make life miserable for everyone including yourself if you fixate on this stuff."

"None of what I'm feeling is valid because Mom and Dad love me and they are good people."

The loudest message that kept playing in my head was a question: "Am I crazy?"

That question—and the incessant googling that accompanied it—eventually led me to an amazing film that changed my life. It was a documentary by Mary Knight called *Am I Crazy? My Journey to Determine if My Memories Are True.*

Finding Mary's film about her own journey with repressed and recovered traumatic memory was yet another awakening for me. As I watched her story, and read her subsequent essays, the answer that came to me was unmistakable: No, she is clearly not crazy. And neither am I. We've just been living in a culture that makes it very risky to acknowledge our feelings and to remember the experiences that triggered those feelings.

I'm grateful to Mary for shining a light on her own truth—and thereby opening a door for others to walk through as well.

Anna Holtzman, LMHC, is a licensed mental health counselor. She is a chronic pain recovery therapist and coach, www.annaholtzman.com.

How I Healed from Fibromyalgia and Trauma-Induced Chronic Pain

Trigger Warning: Low

The Need to Heal

Until I was thirty-two years old, I thought everyone suffered from physical pain all the time. I was sitting in a rocking chair, my younger son on my lap, when I discovered that most people are pain free. I was a member of a group of mothers, and it was my turn to host. My older son, age four, was in his bedroom, trying to endure the required sharing of toys with the other "big kids." Mothers of young children have an easy intimacy, talking nonstop about personal subjects like C-sections and the endless agony of potty training. I mentioned something about my body pain. I was surprised that the other women could not relate. "You mean, you don't have pain anywhere in your body right now?" A woman breastfeeding her two-month-old daughter looked at me with compassion and slowly shook her head. I went around the room, asking multiple questions of each person. I found out that chronic pain is not the norm.

When I tell people about my recovery, they often inquire, "How did you heal?" That question cannot be answered in one or two sentences. Furthermore, the answer that I give is personalized to me. To get well, individuals have to navigate their own healing journey. If you suffer from chronic pain, your recipe for recovery may be quite different from mine.

My essential ingredients for becoming pain free follow. Do not let my long list overwhelm you. These are practices that I have employed over twenty-plus years. It is not humanly possible to do them all at once. Take the ideas that you like and leave the rest. Many of the recovery techniques remain embedded in my life, even now that it is relatively pain free.

Healing modalities require expenditures of time and money. Some may not seem affordable. Try anyway. Do what you can with what you have. If necessary, readjust the family budget. You are worth it. I was in a book group with a highly intelligent woman who was in her early thirties and wheelchair bound. She used to have fibromyalgia. She was working back then and did not think that she had time to spend on her healing. In addition, she and her husband did not have money for it in their household budget. Her health continued to deteriorate. By the time I met her, she had multiple sclerosis (MS) and was on disability, unable to hold a job. Knowing her led me to change my internal value structure. I found that I could not get well until I gave my health top priority.

HOW I HEALED

Healthy Lifestyle Choices

Sleep

Get enough sleep at night. I need nine hours per night. I probably always will.

I still have sleep problems and nightmares. It is my only current post traumatic stress disorder (PTSD) symptom. I have a special pillow, which I take with me wherever I go. I am extremely picky about mattresses when I travel. I call hotels prior to my stay to find out what kind of mattress they have. There are a few hotel chains that I automatically trust, such as Best Western. When I am going to stay in someone else's home, I bring my air mattress. I have an easy-to-pack, high quality one from R.E.I.

I have TMJ (temporomandibular joint) problems. No matter how much body work I receive, I still find wearing a mouth guard essential. I used to need one whenever I took a daytime nap, but now I only need one at night. I hate going to the dentist, and yet I am glad that I have made extra trips to dental offices so that I can wear a mouth guard. I wore the same one for twelve years, even after it was partially broken, because I was unable to find a dentist who could make me a new one that was comfortable enough. I was so dependent on it that I would get more upset when I misplaced my mouth guard than I did when I misplaced my wedding ring! My current dentist was angelic in his patience with me when the first two mouth guards he made caused pain. I am glad that he and I kept trying because my new one fits just right. I have tried using the inexpensive mouth guards that can be purchased at a drug store, but I just wasted my money doing so.

Because of a specific incident of childhood trauma, sometimes my legs get extremely cold at night. When this happens, I wear thermal underwear, even with my flannel night gown or pajamas. I have worn leg warmers at night a few times. A hot water bottle is sometimes helpful. I used to listen to CDs every night as I fell asleep. Now I do so only as needed. I continue to employ every means possible to accommodate my nighttime self.

Healthy Eating

Alone in a twin bed, library books strewn around me, my body throbbing with sharp pain, I researched food recommendations for those suffering from fibromyalgia. The suggestions on what foods to eat and to avoid varied greatly. Some sources endorsed fish "twice weekly" while others forbade all sea food. But there were commonalities, which I followed. Drink plenty of water, eat lots of vegetables, avoid junk food, and gravitate toward whole foods instead of processed items.

Fortunately, I do not drink alcohol or soft drinks, which were forbidden.

I got good at cooking from scratch and created recipes for soups, including a tasty vegan split-pea. (Just rinse split peas, then boil them in tap water and add carrots, green peas, yellow peppers, zucchini, or any other favorite vegetables.)

To avoid sugar, I quit eating traditional sweet desserts and even quit drinking fruit juice. Eating a piece of fruit became a divine treat. My taste buds, no longer deadened by refined substances, could distinguish the subtle differences between varieties of apples, pears, berries, and oranges.

I quit eating chocolate for eleven years. That's how much I value my health!

Purchasing food at a grocery store instead of a restaurant saves money and, at least for me, encourages healthier choices. I limit eating out. For years, no matter where I went, I would pack a sack lunch or dinner in a small ice chest. Shredded wheat and cashew milk remain my go-to foods if I decide to do this and am running late. Some of the foods that I cut out of my diet for a long time are foods that I now savor, like unbleached wheat flour and, thankfully, chocolate!

As I write this, I am eating my usual "dessert." And, yes, I will share the recipe:

1. Cut up a medium-sized apple and then microwave for three minutes.

2. Crumble a small slice of homemade bread into the apple dish.

3. Add a little butter to the mix.

4. Microwave for another thirty seconds.

5. Sprinkle with cinnamon (but no sugar).

As you can tell, my diet continues to be healthy. My body is my wellness guide. I find that when I start eating a lot of refined sugar, my body gets mad, and my chronic pain returns. I eventually heed the complaints filed by my physical self and abstain from all refined sugar for two to four weeks. My taste buds reward me by allowing me to again relish the subtle differences in flavor of every apple and orange that I consume.

Exercise

I have never known anyone who healed from fibromyalgia without exercise. It was hard to exercise when my body was in constant pain, but I am glad that I made myself do so. When I was very sick, I attended an exercise class with people much older than me. I got great emotional support from them.

Yoga

I do yoga almost every day, and I savor it! To make yoga classes affordable, I get a $99 monthly unlimited pass. I know that yoga can always be a part of my life, no matter what physical limitations I might have someday, because there are adaptive classes even for people in wheelchairs. Yoga is not a competitive activity. You do what works best for your body. I have been doing yoga for twenty-seven years, and yet, I usually go to the classes labeled "Gentle Yoga." I have tried various types of yoga. I do not recommend hot yoga (also called Bikram). I went to one class, but I had to leave early because it reminded me of my abuse.

Walking/Hiking

One of my favorite forms of exercise is walking. I rejoice in long walks.

When we were house-hunting and first saw the house where we now live, my husband and I went on a walk while we discussed whether to make an offer on it or not. In less than half a block, we were on a forested path. I knew then that I wanted this house to become our forever home! We can walk almost exclusively on trails to a lake that is two and a half miles from our house. There are beautiful waterfalls a mile beyond the lake.

I hiked with a group from the senior center prior to the pandemic. It was an amazingly active group of seniors. They had three levels of hiking groups, and I was in the medium one. The fast group was not only too rigorous, but they did not stop long enough for lunch. I am transfixed by the view at the top of a mountain.

Early in the pandemic, I made a commitment to walk/hike ten to twenty miles each week. I love doing this! I can clear my mind by walking a few miles alone, but there are also benefits to having a companion. Some of my closest friends through the years have been my walking buddies.

Nick Sadigh with Bellingham Media Group

HOW I HEALED

Other Fun Activities

Dance

Dancing is its own category of fun! The first few times my husband and I danced together, we took it seriously. We even took dance lessons. Eventually, we resolved to use dance simply as a silly pastime. We hold each other and sway back and forth in ways that feel good, with or without music playing. Once I heard a song that I liked over the loudspeaker in a Walmart store. I took my husband in my arms, and we waltzed down an aisle, laughing.

For me, dance can be a way to communicate with God. A meditative dance instructor named Gabriel Roth wrote the book *Sweat Your Prayers: Movement as Spiritual Practice.* The approach Roth created includes five rhythms. I went to a "Sweat Your Prayers" class once. It was wonderful. I swirled fervently and sweated. It was obvious that anything goes. I decided that I wanted to lay flat on the ground. The feet of the other dancers beat on the hardwood floor so intensely that, with my ear to the ground, I heard drumming. Fingers touching the floor, I felt its movement. I tasted my own tears. I was in heaven! I returned once. Why not many more times? Looking back, I think it was because I could stand only so much joy back then. I was married to my first husband, and fear was a background noise in my everyday existence.

Recently, during the isolation of the COVID pandemic, I attended ecstatic dance classes online. One is aptly named "Dance Church." I find joy in the energy of dancing with others, but I also love to create a private oasis. I close my curtains, plug in my CD player, put on a favorite song, and just move. Alone in my bedroom, I might even take my clothes off!

Play

I crave play! Doesn't everyone? And yet, I have a hard time finding free-spirited adults, which is one reason that I like hanging out with kids. For example, several years ago I realized that I did not have enough children in my life, so I hosted a neighborhood Halloween costume contest in my front yard.

I started collecting dolls early in my recovery. I splurged on a soft-bodied baby doll. Sitting in a rocking chair, holding this doll to my heart, I healed a young part of myself. Knowing how much it would mean to me, a friend gave me an unusual birthday present one year. It was the brown eyed doll she had treasured since childhood.

I adore children's books and sometimes check them out from the library just for me. At a survivor conference, stretched out on the floor after an intense workshop, another attendee and I took turns reading children's books to each other.

Out of a sense of lightheartedness, I have tried a few things that were not for me in the long run. I remember being so proud of my first ballet shoes, at age forty-two! After I took one set of classes, I kept the pink shoes as a keepsake. I have had one, and only one, private tutoring lesson in gymnastics, clowning, belly dancing, and aerial yoga. Play was sometimes scary for me as a child, but I have definitely reclaimed my exuberant nature as an adult.

Creativity

My pain used to be so bad that I did not want a long life. However, even with my worst pain, in the midst of writing something that I knew only I could write, I was happy, and I wanted to live forever. My creative life is something that I always will cherish. One of the essays in this memoir, "The Magic of Creativity," gives a behind-the-scenes look at my filmmaking, writing, and other creative endeavors.

Voice Lessons

I took a voice lesson so that I could learn how to sing, but I found that what I really needed to learn was to breathe. I was quite young when I taught myself not to breathe deeply. Inflating the deepest part of my abdomen terrorizes an infantile part of me. Consequently, I so appreciate the kind instruction that I receive via Zoom from Allison Pelot of Pure Energy PDX (www.pureenergypdx.com). My shoulders sink as I relax into my visceral glimpses of the magical power of deep breathing.

I never have met Allison in person. We both attended an

incredible two-day global online workshop for women called Vocal Odyssey (www.vocalodyssey.com). The instructor, Nessi Gomes, states, "Vocal Odyssey is a deep yet playful self-inquiry journey of discovery into the mystery and healing forces of our most intimate musical instrument—our voice. The process aims to pierce through the voices in our heads and to open a door for a new relationship between us and the transformative quality of our vocal expression." I paid about $100 to attend, and it was definitely worth it. Supported by women from around the world, I played, I cried, and I made lots of noise.

Many years ago, I took my first singing lessons from the elderly, warm-hearted choir leader of the Methodist church that I attended. He tried to persuade me to do breathing exercises, but the Barbie doll rigidity I maintained back then would not accommodate them. I never got good enough to sing in the choir, but I did start to appreciate my own voice. I would dance around my bedroom, giggling while singing Christmas carols. My pitch is noticeably better with carols than with hymns because they do not remind me of my childhood. I sang hymns as a child when my father led singing at our church. The other members of our church celebrated Christmas in their homes, but my parents referred to it as a pagan holiday and disallowed its observance. When there were Christmas parties in my classroom at school, I had to sit in the principal's office until the party was over. As an adult, I had fun learning the words to well-known jingles.

During my twenty-plus years' break from voice lessons, I progressed in healing my voice through my participation in an organization dedicated to improving public speaking and communication skills. In Toastmasters, I honed my vocal variety, meaning changes in pitch, pace, and/or volume. Like many of my fellow Toastmasters, I joined out of necessity after blowing a work-related presentation. I am glad that I continued even after achieving an acceptable level of effectiveness. Winning a humorous speech contest helped me to be confident enough to eventually become a filmmaker. Toastmasters clubs are affordable and are available globally (www.toastmasters.org).

Art

The first professional artist whom I befriended is someone I knew before I started my recovery process. Donna Howell Sickles, known for her cowgirl art, lived in my hometown of Frisco, Texas, when it had a population of about 7,000. She took charge of the elementary school's PTA art contest each year. One day, after the step aerobics class we took together, Donna asked me to help with the art contest. My life had just been shattered by recovering memories of my childhood molestation. I had decided not to do any volunteer work unless it very directly benefitted one of my sons. (I never quit being a homeroom mom.) I told Donna why I was declining to volunteer, and she listened with compassion. Not long after that, I realized that art was a necessary component of my healing. Tired and sweaty after a vigorous aerobics class, I went through a lengthy explanation as I asked Donna for advice. She replied, "What medium are you drawn to?" I thought that she did not understand my request, but she did. She said that I would heal best by using whatever appealed to me most, whether sculpting, painting, drawing, or making collages. I told her that I wanted to paint. She asked, "Thin paint or thick paint?" We figured out that what I really wanted to do was finger paint. It was no coincidence that I was drawn to finger painting. Donna told me that thick paint and large brushes heighten emotional responses. (Art supplies like colored pencils tend to bring out less affect.) Back then, I had difficulty unlocking my deep feelings.

I drove my SUV home, determined to immediately follow Donna's suggestions, and yet nervous about the heartbreak that might bleed out. Still, I mixed several colors. When my sons were preschoolers, I started making finger paint for them by combining equal portions of dry tempera paint and dishwashing liquid, which makes cleanup easy.

Art from a class I took in 2012

That is what I did for myself. Donna had cautioned me that the larger the drawing, the more emotion it is likely to elicit. I knew that I needed the largest paper possible! Moving stores sell boxes of packing paper at a good price, and I had some under my bed from when my sons were younger. I sat down at my dining table and painted a pretty picture of a house and trees, then smothered it with dark blobs of paint. I spent ten minutes making angry art. With paint-covered fingers, I wrote hateful messages to my per-petrators. I made stick figures of them with disgusting faces and amputated limbs. When I got tired, I sat for a couple of minutes, catching my breath. I ate a graham cracker and drank a glass of milk. Then I put the disturbing artwork away and started painting a pastel house with glowing windows. Strong green trees stood under sunny skies, and lots of flowers surrounded the house. I used a paint-covered finger to write kind messages to myself. I hung this happy art in my bedroom. To my ex-husband's credit, he allowed our bedroom to be adorned with my creative treasures.

I still heal through art. For less messy art sessions, I use crayons, pencils, and coloring books. I am glad that coloring books for adults are now available, but I often use ones designed for children. I used to cut out paper dolls. I would sit up in bed, relaxing as I carefully trimmed clothes for each doll. I have done various other crafts. I adore painting little wooden ornaments and boxes that I get from Michaels. Sometimes I paint with the children whom I foster or babysit, but when I sit by myself on an old shower curtain littered with containers of acrylic paint, I feel a unique joy.

I have taken a few private art therapy sessions, but finding a good art therapist has been difficult, especially one who will take my health insurance. I have discovered that it is therapeutic for me to simply do art on my own and then bring my creation to the next session with my psychotherapist.

Recently I started attending art therapy classes online through HUSH No More, a 501(c)3 nonprofit organization founded in 2019 to provide a platform for survivors to share their experiences (www.hushnomore.org). These classes are for women and are available free of charge to attendees from all over the world. Anyone who has suffered any kind of trauma is eligible to attend.

Reading

During some of my hardest times, books were my best friends. For a number of years, I diligently studied self-help books. I occasionally read them now, but most of the time, I read just for fun. Curled up in a comfy chair, snuggled under my cotton quilt, I read novels and short stories. Sometimes I feel like I learn as much from the characters in novels as I did from examining self-help books. Liane Moriarty, best known for her book and subsequent mini-series *Big Little Lies*, seems to have a deep understanding of the dynamics involved in domestic violence. As a teenager and as an adult, I devoured *A Tree Grows in Brooklyn* by Betty Smith multiple times, always gaining a new perspective. When a book is triggering, I often skip sections to find how it ends. I give myself full permission to do so. Reading should not cause misery! I often go back to the book and read it in its entirety, just out of order.

I like short stories that I can read in a single sitting. The short stories of Alice Munro are especially insightful. When I am depressed, I reread "Dimensions," the first story in Munro's book *Too Much Happiness*. It is a tragic tale, which I find oddly uplifting. I adored *Paris for One and Other Stories* by Jojo Moyes. The book *Everyday People: The Color of Life—A Short Story Anthology*, edited by Jennifer Baker, contains fascinating viewpoints via its diversity of writers. There are occasions, though, when I am not interested in stimulating my mind. On a scratchy-throat, drizzly-outside, temperature-turned-up-inside, herbal-tea sort of day, I found the ideal way to entertain myself. I gobbled up *The Unhoneymooners* by Christina Lauren and learned absolutely nothing.

I check out books from the library incessantly. I put new books on hold instead of purchasing them, even if I need to wait a few months to read them. I find that it is usually faster to obtain large print editions. I have decided that, since I use the library so much, an occasional late fee or lost book is reasonable. If I am charged a fine, I think of it as a user fee, not as a penalty.

HOW I HEALED

Spiritual Practices

Spirituality

It is difficult to summarize this source of strength and happiness since spirituality has been a visceral experience for me since early childhood. At age six, after being injured in a cruel assault, I had what I consider to be either a near-death experience or a vision. I could literally see, taste, and touch God's love. I was raised in a church that told of a judgement-oriented God. A Bible passage that was used to reinforce this concept reads, "Work out your own salvation with fear and trembling." I realized when I was young that I had a natural tendency to want to be kind to other people. I did not understand why there was a need for "fear and trembling" since I already wanted to be good. At age twelve, I read the Bible from cover to cover for the first of many times. I memorized whole chapters. The words reinforced my belief in a God of compassion and comfort. As I explain in the essay "My Relationship with Religion," my priority regarding Bible study has changed drastically. I still see God through the eyes and heart of my child self.

Meditation/Prayer

I am never at my best unless I am meditating daily. I use the word meditation for what others would describe as prayer. Each day, I try to clear my mind and allow communication between myself and the divine. (When using the word "divine," I am aware that it could be replaced with a number of other terms, including God, my higher power, my best self, the deepest part of my heart, or my true intention.) I believe that God communicates with me when I empty my mind.

I choose between types of meditation. Sometimes it is sitting meditation, journaling, or quiet hikes. Lately it has been a meditative type of yoga called Yin. In Yin, you hold a relaxing yoga pose for three to six minutes. I have a specific Yin yoga routine that I do at home. I have memorized the sequence. I set the timer on my phone and sink into each pose, allowing my mind to unburden itself.

Early in my recovery, I enjoyed meditation retreats. The longest one that I attended lasted five days. It was much easier to practice silence in a group setting. A couple of times when I was not at a retreat, I found friends who wanted to eat a meal with me in silence. These gatherings reminded me of a meditation retreat, and they were free!

Meditation CDs and Downloads

It is hard to start a meditation practice, and sometimes it is hard to keep one going. If I cannot discipline myself to do any other type of meditation, I sit or lay in a quiet room for an hour a day and listen to a recorded meditation via CD or MP3 download.

Holosync advertises that its CDs will enable you to "meditate as deeply as a Zen monk, but eight times faster." Normally I would not pay attention to a claim like that, but since my acupuncturist recommended it, I purchased the introductory package in 2005. I listened to the meditation session known as "The Dive and Immersion" daily for the next few years. I still listen to it occasionally and find it helpful. My hesitation in recommending this tool is its cost. The introductory package cost me $99 and included two other beneficial recorded meditations ("Quietude" and "Making Change Easy"). I have noticed that the price has fluctuated over time. At one point, the introductory package cost $500. The last time I checked, though, it had been reduced to $179. I am glad that I purchased what I did, and I am glad that I did not purchase the rest of the series, which is much more expensive. A friend loaned me the other levels, but I decided that my Level One CDs were all that I wanted. To purchase Holosync CDs, go to www. centerpointe.com.

Bella Ruth Nappersack CDs are wonderful and reasonably priced! She adapts them for specific issues. I especially like the ones on fibromyalgia, post traumatic stress disorder (PTSD), restful sleep, anger/forgiveness, and depression. For more information about them, go to www.healthjourneys.com.

HOW I HEALED

Support Groups

Social Media

I am in two private Facebook groups with fellow child abuse survivors. One is specifically for sex trafficking survivors. Sometimes, I crave support from people who had childhoods like mine. Other times, I want to be embraced by people with whom I have non-abuse-related shared interests.

Twelve-Step Groups

Al-Anon is one of the best sources of group support (www. al-anon.org). It is free and readily available worldwide. Anyone who has a relative or friend with a drinking problem can attend. Alcohol abuse is such a common problem that I have never met anyone who does not qualify for Al-Anon. Many people qualify for more than one type of the many twelve-step programs. Incest Survivors Anonymous can be especially valuable. In any twelve-step group, keep going to meetings until you find one that is a good fit. I have heard one way to judge if you are in the right place is to make sure there is as much laughter as there are tears.

I have not been going to Al-Anon for the last few months, but I am still on the local Al-Anon group's email list. Knowing when and where the meetings are is a type of emotional insurance for me.

Domestic Violence Groups for Women

I am sure that I never would have gotten well had I stayed

married to the father of my children. This marriage included verbal abuse, as well as something that could be considered physical abuse. My ex-husband would poke me to get my attention. This might have been just annoying rather than physically painful had it not been for my fibromyalgia. I would ask him to call my name instead, or touch my arm, but he would "forget." I sometimes wonder if I should have left sooner. I never wonder if I should have stayed longer.

A week after I left my twenty-three-year marriage, I started attending domestic violence classes for women. At the first class, I did not think that I fit with the other women. They had endured horrendous beatings. I am glad that I kept attending. I soon learned that everyone in the room had been subjected to verbal abuse and considered it one of the most destructive types of marital violence.

Deciding whether to divorce or not is hard no matter what the circumstances. If you are a victim of any form of domestic violence, seek help. I consider group support essential when leaving an abusive relationship. *One Man's Anger, One Woman's Love*, a short film that I made to help fellow survivors of marital abuse, is available free on my website and YouTube channel. Spanish subtitles are available.

Grief Classes and Groups

I went to a class at a church on grief shortly after my divorce. The teacher had a huge amount of empathy for each participant, no matter what type of loss they had endured. She told us that, after her son died, she was never able to find her car keys. She found a purse with a car key attachment. For the next ten years, I bought purses with devices for attaching keys. I no longer need a purse like this, but it helped for many years. Grief support in a group setting might be available through your local hospice organization, place of worship, or community center.

Rape Crisis Center Groups

I attended a support group at a rape crisis center. It was free. It was for any woman who had ever been raped. Some participants had been raped as adults, and some, as children. We definitely had enough in common to relate to one another.

HOW I HEALED

Psychotherapy

Finding the Right Psychotherapist

Psychotherapy has been vital to my recovery. I have been
in psychotherapy off and on as needed, rather than contin-
uously. I am a survivor of extreme child abuse. My childhood exploitation was so traumatic that my mind allowed
me to hide all knowledge of it from myself until, at age
thirty-seven, I felt safe enough to remember it. I could not
have processed my recovered memories without therapeutic intervention because I would not have felt safe enough
to do so. My psychotherapist held a nurturing, supportive
space for me as I dealt with the emotional content of my
memories. I received an email recently from a thirty-two-
year-old woman who had recalled the severe abuse that
occurred throughout her childhood. She wanted my advice
but said that she does not trust counselors. She told about
a bad experience that she had with a therapist. I hope that
she will reconsider counseling. I offered her a free telephone
call with me so that we could talk about it. So far, I have not
heard back from her. The paradox is that it is hard to trust
people when you have had horrendous experiences like
mine, but it also may be impossible to recover from these
experiences unless you find someone who is a trustworthy
guide.

I have heard that it is as hard to find a psychotherapist
who is right for you as to find a marital partner. Keep trying!
I am glad I did. I now am happy with my therapist (and, for
that matter, with my awesome husband). I encourage you to

keep searching until you find a psychotherapist whom you trust. There are many counselors who are not good, but I always have been able to eventually find one who is helpful.

If you are low income and do not have adequate health insurance, your struggle will be harder. My hope for you is that you will find an agency with affordable services. I know some excellent counselors who work for organizations with sliding-scale fees.

There is a free self-help recovery group that might be beneficial while you are looking for a professional counselor. It is sponsored by the National Association of Adult Survivors of Child Abuse (NAASCA). It is led by a survivor who has appropriate training. Currently, it meets via Zoom several times a week. For more information, go to their website: www.naasca.org.

I am less dependent on therapists than I was earlier in my recovery, but I still consider at least occasional psychotherapy essential to my well-being. My current psychotherapist is excellent. Counseling sessions every other week via Zoom help me stay calm (even during a pandemic). It feels to me like a conversation with a good friend, except it is always my turn to talk!

Types of Psychotherapy

I have profited from traditional "talk" therapy, EMDR (eye movement), brain spotting (similar to EMDR), hypnosis, progressive muscle relaxation, and couple's counseling. In 2018, I discovered a type of body-oriented psychotherapy. I traveled to Leipzig, Germany, for a screening of my first documentary. There I met German psychologist Dr. Ralf Vogt. Dr. Vogt, along with his wife, Irina, who is also a psychologist, developed a novel therapy technique and designed fascinating equipment to implement it. (Books that he has

written about *SIM 30*, which is what he calls this type of
therapy, have been translated into English and are available on Amazon.) I felt like a treasured child as I scram-
bled onto an adult-sized rocking horse. There was a huge,
very sturdy, womb-like enclosure big enough for me and
my husband to crawl into. My favorite experience, though,
was being swayed back and forth by Dr. Vogt without him
physically touching me. A soft blanket was placed over the
already well-cushioned surface of a giant red barrel. I sunk
into it and relaxed fully for the first time since arriving in
Germany. I was later told that the barrel has metal wires
inside so that my own heartbeat was echoed back to me.
It was easy to imagine being so young that I had not yet
been born. I asked if I could have an on-camera counseling session and, unlike other therapists who declined such a
request, Dr. Vogt agreed to it. Within this session, I released
anger toward my perpetrators and received comfort from
the part of me that provides parenting to my adult self.
This footage appears near the end of my documentary
Mothers and Molestation: A Film about Child Abuse.

When I returned home, I tried to find a body-oriented
psychotherapist to continue this type of healing. I could
not find anyone in the town where I live. Since I had to
travel ninety miles to find one, I booked a double session.
This session was quite different from the one with Dr. Vogt,
and yet I found it beneficial. However, I have not returned. I
postponed receiving this type of psychotherapy because of
the pandemic. Also, I am unsure if I still need it.

Marriage Counseling

I am happily married, but not every minute of every day.
My wonderful husband, Jerry, does not like marriage counseling. (He reports that he is "neutral" toward it.) Early in

our marriage, we went to a communication class. When we use the "I" statement skills that we were taught, we find that we can solve most problems on our own. Still, periodically I insist on a couple's session. More than once I have, not so kindly, reminded Jerry that prior to our marriage, he promised that he would always be willing to get marriage counseling. Jerry's compromise is to participate in up to six sessions per year, which is always enough. At one point in our marriage, when we were having trouble getting along, a counselor made a simple suggestion. We were assigned to take turns planning a weekly date. Spending fun time together on a regular basis reminds us of how much we love each other.

Sexual Healing

For me, sex is good only when it is an expression of love in its purest form. Being married to my husband Jerry has enabled me to heal sexually. Like most people, Jerry likes sex. And yet, he never pressures me. Early in our marriage, I confided to my best friend about something that was bothering me. I told her that Jerry and I did not have sex very often. Jerry was hurt that I talked to her about it instead of to him. I said, "But you know we don't have sex much." He said, "Yes, but I didn't know that you were upset about it." Then Jerry added, "We make love all the time. We cuddle every night." I am fortunate to be married to a man who considers cuddling a form of love making. We have sex more often now, but Jerry still places more value on making me happy than on his own desires. I do not know how to have sex with someone who does not love me with his whole heart, nor do I want to know.

I have recommendations for sexual healing that do not involve a partner. Rape survivor Wendy Maltz wrote *The*

Sexual Healing Journey: A Guide for Sexual Abuse Survivors. This book provides exercises that progress toward sexual touch. However, it begins with touch that is not erotic and does not lead to sex. Some of the exercises can be done with a partner. I read this book for the first time many years ago, early in my recovery. I was unable to do some of the exercises at that time.

Because of my childhood trauma, I used to be terrified of solo sex. I felt inconsolably lonely when I tried to touch myself sexually. I am not talking about loneliness in the usual sense of the word. It was as though I was condemned to decades of solitary confinement. On an intellectual basis, I believed, as I do now, that masturbation is completely normal, wholesome, and healthy. Nevertheless, I could have pleasurable, orgasmic, spiritually enriching solo sex only after I went to a sex coach. Upon my psychotherapist's recommendation and with the support of my wonderful husband, Jerry, I went to Amy Weissfeld (joyfulselflove. com). I see solo sex as a form of commitment to my deepest self. It is a time when I allow myself to feel adored by God. I agree with the statement on Amy's website: "Pleasure is our birthright."

HOW I HEALED

Physical Therapy and Other Body Work

Physical Therapy

I consider physical therapists the geniuses of our time! More than once, at a crucial time in my healing process, a physical therapist has done what appeared to me to be high-level detective work to determine the source of my pain. This information was used to develop my individualized exercise program, which was then tweaked if any of the suggested activities resulted in additional pain.

I continue to go to physical therapy at least a few times a year. I try to do the recommended exercises on a regular basis. Returning to the physical therapist annually helps me keep this commitment.

Do not let anyone make you feel bad if you do not get well as quickly as most patients. If you are released from treatment too soon, as I have been on multiple occasions, just keep doing the exercises you were given, and pursue whatever alternative treatment you can afford.

Pelvic Floor Physical Therapy (Also Known as Women's Health Physical Therapy)

A pelvic floor physical therapist treats the area of the body that a gynecologist is trained to examine. Pelvic floor muscles are located between the tailbone and the pubic bone. They support the bladder, bowel, uterus, and vagina. Pelvic floor physical therapists can be helpful to both men and women.

When I took childbirth classes, I learned the importance of Kegel exercises and did them twice a day as recommended by the teacher. Sprawled on my earth tone sofa, trying my best to relax, I combatted such excruciating pain that I had to use my childbirth breath training. I now know that I had severe vaginal scarring. Prior to gaining this knowledge, I thought everyone had an asymmetrical vaginal wall like mine. I no longer have any vaginal scarring thanks to the treatment I received and the self-treatment that I was taught.

Educating others about pelvic floor physical therapy is important because many chronic pain sufferers have never heard of it. Some rape survivors confide that they are hesitant to try it, even after being advised to do so by their trusted medical doctor.

I found out about pelvic floor physical therapy by accident. In 2003, the physical therapist whom I had seen multiple times was coaching me as I lay on the floor doing a clam shell knee lift exercise. I had a sharp pain. I looked up at her and told her that I thought I should wait on that exercise until I could figure out in psychotherapy the cause of pain. I described my experience with Kegels. She said, "There's a type of physical therapy that addresses that." I made my first pelvic floor physical therapist appointment before leaving her office, but when I got back into my car, I looked at my scheduling book and figured out a reason to postpone it. I was nervous! I called the receptionist. Before I hung up, I decided to ask that the pelvic floor physical therapist call me to answer some questions. The receptionist asked me to hold. I had no time to think of specific questions. The woman who would become my first pelvic floor physical therapist was in the office. When she came to the phone, I muttered, "I'm really nervous." I do not remember any of her words, but I still can hear the compassionate understanding with which she said them.

I have received pelvic floor physical therapy since 2003. I have been treated by a total of six therapists, all of whom have been highly competent and completely respectful.

Video clips of interviews with my current pelvic floor physical therapist are available on my YouTube channel. Titles include "Common Reasons for Pelvic Floor Physical Therapy" and "Are Kegel Exercises Ever Harmful?"

Massage

I relish a good massage. Years ago, I promised my body that, even after getting completely well, I would get massages on a regular basis. One reason that I made this promise to myself was that I had heard that if chronic pain benefits you in any way, your subconscious may conspire against your attempts to heal. I get a massage at least twice a month. It is my favorite luxury. I love my massage therapist (but not in a way that would make my husband jealous!).

Cranial sacral, visceral manipulation, Swedish, Hawaiian, Thai, trigger point, and reflexology all are magnificent! I no longer do Rolfing, but the partial series that I had helped me. I go to both male and female massage therapists and have had great results from both. Recently, I went to a massage therapist while traveling. Since I had not met this therapist before, I asked her to limit the massage to my hands, arms, and feet. She respected my wishes. When I am at an airport on a layover, I often get a chair massage.

The problem with massage is the cost. I am willing to give up many other things to afford this treatment. I would rather have a massage each month than go out to eat. I bought a massage table years ago. An adjustable table makes massage more comfortable for the person giving it, as well as for the receiver. When I was single and on a tight budget, I traded giving and receiving massages with female friends. A few years ago, my pelvic floor physical therapist taught my husband to give the type of massage that I had been receiving from her. He got good at it.

MELT (www.meltmethod.com) is a self-massage technique that helps me. The equipment is expensive, but it is a one-time expense. I think that the expense it is worth it if and only if you are going to use it on a regular basis.

I could not have gotten well without massage, and I cannot stay well without it.

Acupuncture

Throughout my healing journey, acupuncture has helped. I find my progress is dependent on having a good relationship with the acupuncturist. I have been to a dozen acupuncturists through the years. All but one were effective. The ineffective one was very clinical and not particularly caring. I tend to need extra time with the needles in, and I have found that most acupuncturists will allow this.

I tried herbal remedies recommended by acupuncturists a couple of times. They did not seem beneficial. I admit that I did not continue these treatments for long because I did not like the smell or taste of them.

Many of my acupuncture treatments have been covered by my health insurance. Group acupuncture treatment is more affordable than private sessions. At a survivor conference that I attended, acupuncture was offered free of charge in a group setting. This was my sole experience with group acupuncture, and it was sensational!

HOW I HEALED

Medication

Antidepressants

I started taking antidepressants in 1995, and I still take them daily. My dosage changes depending on the stress in my life, and it is lower now than it used to be. I initially was extremely hesitant to go on any medication. A few years after I recovered memories of my childhood abuse, I went to the doctor for sleep problems caused by a condition known as "restless leg syndrome." I would wake up at night with a sensation in the muscles of my right leg. I felt fatigued, like I had been riding a bike or running. I was prescribed an extremely low dose of antidepressant. It was the third time a primary care physician had suggested that I try antidepressants. I discussed it with my psychologist, who, in turn, persuaded me to take my doctor's advice. I started sleeping better. Soon after that, I started taking a normal dosage of the antidepressant. That was almost thirty years ago. I have been on antidepressants ever since.

I tried to go off them about ten years ago, and I noticed a tendency toward sadness. I might take antidepressants the rest of my life. They work for me, and I am no longer ashamed that I need them.

Other Medication

In the past, anti-anxiety medication was helpful to me. I no longer take it. If you do take anti-anxiety medication, please use it sparingly. I know many people who have become addicted to it. I had withdrawal symptoms when I quit using it.

Medical marijuana was not helpful to me. It just made me tired. I used pain medication for a short time at as low a dosage as possible. Pain medication will never cure you. Commitment to a healthy lifestyle will.

Nick Sadigh with Bellingham Media Group

HOW I HEALED

Social Interactions

Balanced Friendships

The people who are now a part of my life add to my everyday happiness. I have cut ties with all the individuals who hurt me.

Quit friendships that are draining. In the past, there were times when it seemed as though I was the unpaid counselor for many of my friends. I must admit that my addiction to helping others was a major factor in this. It felt good to seek out people who needed something from me. I did not adhere to this wise saying, "A friend is one who overlooks your broken fence and admires the flowers in your garden." I now have balanced friendships, even with people who do not have the health and financial security with which I am now blessed. I no longer monopolize conversations with my unsolicited advice on fence repair. One of my favorite activities is to talk on the phone to a friend for an hour or two while walking on a forested path, breathing in glimpses of treetops and feeling girlfriend love.

As I grow older, the ages of my friends do not change. I delight in becoming friends with both elderly individuals and children. From my maternal grandmother, a relative who never abused me, I learned the importance of friendships with young people. Nanny lived well into her nineties. When she started making ceramics at age fifty, she joined a ceramics club with women twenty to thirty years younger than her. Unlike her peers, these women were available to her late in life. Once a month, when the ceramics club met for a potluck, I always knew where Nanny would be.

Women's groups are a treasured part of my life. I am currently in two book clubs. I have luscious discussions about novels (and, also, more personal matters) with the other women in my clubs. I used to be in a group called SISTERS through a church I attended. We met once a month in a home of one of the members, and the host had carte blanche to choose the topic for the month. Once we were assigned to bring a doll and tell why we chose her. At another meeting, we described the best birthday party that we had ever attended. A few times, before our formal meeting, I sat on a sofa alone, listening to indistinguishable sounds from various conversations. When I think back on it, I can still taste the joy of the familial companionship.

Limiting Volunteer Activities

Limit volunteer activities, including what you do for family and friends. I quit all volunteer work for two years after I recovered my childhood memories. I am normally extremely earthfriendly, but I even made a conscious decision to quit recycling. Each time I threw something in the trash that could have been recycled, I reminded my soul of its importance.

Finding Family

Incest demolishes families. Some survivors find it desirable to rebuild some level of relationship with their biological kin. I chose a different path. I feel great about the family I have now. Other than my relationships with sons and grandchildren, and sporadic emails from one cousin, I have no contact with anyone biologically connected to me. None of the women I proudly refer to as my sisters share my genetics. I discuss more details about whom I now consider family in my "Family" essay.

I was a guest speaker on the Stop Child Abuse Now Blog-TalkRadio show. Those who called in to listen were asked to identify themselves by their name (real or assumed) and their actual geographical location. Multiple countries were represented. The host of the show was father/daughter incest survivor Penelope Bemis. She and I were excited to find out that we live just ninety miles from each other and that we both enjoy yoga and hiking. As soon as the show ended, we arranged to meet in person.

When we got together, Penelope and I talked about our abuse histories briefly. Our focus was on the happy parts of our current lives. Penelope told about her creative ideas for the high school graduation party that she was planning for her son. It was during the pandemic. As a consequence, the guest list would be small. We stayed in touch as much as our busy schedules allowed. We had a quick chat three days before the graduation party. Penelope said that several guests had suddenly cancelled. Penelope's mother, a widow, decided that she did not believe that Penelope was sexually abused and, therefore, would not attend her grandson's graduation party. Penelope's siblings followed suit. The party was boycotted, not solely by this honor student's grandmother, but also by his aunts, uncles, and cousins. I sympathized with Penelope, knowing how hard she had worked on this celebration. I asked if Penelope might like to have me be her pretend sister for the day. She loved the idea! When my husband and I walked up to Penelope's handsomely decorated home bearing a small gift for a teenager whom we had not yet met, we were greeted as family. Fantastic homemade Greek food topped off the afternoon.

I could not imagine anyone willingly missing out on this event.

Holiday Survival Skills

In November of 1994, the wife of our pastor noticed that I was sad about the upcoming holidays. I told her that I was an incest survivor and had broken contact with my parents and siblings to ensure the safety of my children. She alluded to the possibility that I, my sons, and husband (now ex-husband) could come over to their house for Thanksgiving dinner. Even today I can feel my shoulders relaxing as I remember hearing her words! The next week, the pastor came up to me and said that they would have a family-only dinner because they found out that more relatives were coming. In a preacher tone, he said, "Since you need something to do that day, I suggest helping at a homeless shelter." He was clueless about how homeless I already felt. That is when I knew that I needed to develop holiday survival skills.

I am the kind of person who naturally gives more than I get. I had Christmas presents for half of the members of my family of origin when I decided that I needed to break contact with them. It was just June.

I was bitterly lonely in 1993, the first year that I was no longer in contact with my family. In 1994, I bought myself a Christmas present, found some gorgeous wrapping paper, and listened to Mariah Carey music while securing the present with colorful ribbons. Whenever I walked by our Christmas tree and saw the gift, for a glimmer of a moment, I felt like a well-cared for child. I started buying "to me, from me" gifts earlier and earlier in the year until, eventually, I scurried to after-Christmas sales to purchase gifts for the next year. That way I could store these artfully adorned boxes in the holiday decoration storage container. The next Christmas, I would be surprised when opening them.

Back then, greeting card displays in stores made me sad. Throughout my life, I had found ways to make birthdays special for my sister, brothers, and parents. Sometimes, after breaking contact with our parents, I sent my siblings cards. They never reciprocated. One day, standing in a store with tears in my eyes, I decided to get a birthday card for myself. Thus began my year-round practice of shopping for birthday cards for me. Sometimes I would send myself three or four cards. I soon learned that you need to use a USPS drop box rather than mail the card from your own mailbox. Otherwise, you confuse your postal carrier!

I realized that I had finally perfected the art of happy holidaying without relatives on Christmas Day 2021. Our foster son, who I will call Joe, was with us for the sixth time. We do short-term foster care, and Joe stays with us between long-term placements when he has no other place to live. This was his longest visit, having arrived at our door in October, with sad blue eyes peeking through stylishly bleached blond hair. He had been removed from the foster parents who gave him the cool haircut, as well as from the foster parents prior to that, for reasons that had absolutely nothing to do with his behavior.

Joe woke me up at 4:55 on Christmas morning exclaiming, "Grandma, Santa already came!" He insists on calling us his grandparents even though we have no biological connection to him. At age twelve, it could be Joe's last year to believe in Santa. He was ecstatic that Santa ate the homemade chocolate frosting that we left out. Also, did you know that reindeer like Skittles candy? We were indeed right when we told Joe that there was no need for a special Christmas Eve trip to procure candy canes! Upon Joe's request, my Jewish husband was able to surprise Santa by taking a photo of him. The photo was blurry, of course, because Santa was in a rush.

Joe was pleased with his presents, but he had already told me that he was most excited about what was planned for the next day. A couple wanted to adopt him and would take him on an outing on December 26th. It was a white Christmas, and the snow kept falling. I took a long nap while my husband and Joe sledded. At noon, Joe knocked on my door, sorrowful. He said, "I'm scared the roads will keep getting worse, and everyone will be snowed in tomorrow." I knew just what to do. We packed up and drove an hour to a motel with an indoor swimming pool, located just two miles from Joe's new home. After playtime in the pool and a McDonald's dinner, Joe and my husband went to bed early. I sat in our suite, reflecting on my joy-filled Christmas Day. I was so happy that I could not quit smiling. At 10 p.m., my phone rang, and that is when I remembered that I had not talked to my sons or their children all day.

HOW I HEALED

Internal Realizations

Acceptance

As I look at the items in this essay, I realize I will be honored to have them as my travel companions and cherished friends for the rest of my life. My life is, in some ways, richer because of the chronic pain I experienced.

Coming to Terms with Abuse

I am glad that I stayed angry as long as I did because that was what I needed. I used to call forgiveness the "F" word. Confronting abusers helped me, but only because I was careful that I had the physical safety and the emotional support that I needed when I did so. I believe the only person you need to "forgive" is yourself.

I have reached a place that could be called forgiveness with both of my parents. With my father, I simply acknowledge that God is, and has always been, my only father. I now consider myself my own mother, and I acknowledge the fact that I am an amazingly good mother. I am the kind of mother whom I deserve to have, so I am careful to take time to nurture myself.

To those who want to consider completely letting go of their relationship with a parent or both parents, as I did, I recommend the book *Divorcing a Parent: Free Yourself from the Past and Live the Life You've Always Wanted* by Beverly Engel. I have read it several times. The first time was in 1994, and the most recent was last month, while preparing to write this essay. When we divorce our parents, we go against societal messages. As a consequence, we need lots of support.

Health Expectations

Do not expect perfect health. Like almost everyone, I sometimes suffer from illnesses, like colds. I still have minor pain. This discomfort usually resides in either my right hip or right shoulder. Through the years, three different people reported to me that they had fully recovered from fibromyalgia. Each of them promoted a unique remedy, saying that it would work for everyone. All three had their debilitating symptoms reappear, either months or years later. I find that people who truly heal from chronic pain never claim they know a universal cure.

Chronic pain recovery therapist and coach Anna Holtzman acknowledges that she still experiences mild headaches. She states, "I used to get very wound up about whether or not to take a painkiller. I'd judge myself as a 'failure' and worry that I was doing the 'wrong' thing for my healing. Since I let go of those judgments and worries, I stopped having full-blown migraines. I still get twinges when I'm stressed, but the pain maxes out at moderate. Here's what shifted for me: I changed my goal from reducing pain to reducing fear. When I'm having a twinge or a flare, I ask myself what I can do to ease my fear. It's about supporting myself, not punishing myself. It's about feeling better, not about getting a gold star for perfection."

Avoiding the News

I do not watch the nightly news. Hearing about tragedies that I cannot help to alleviate is unduly upsetting to me and serves no purpose. As a little girl, sitting on a scratchy sofa in front of a black and white television screen, I would cry when I saw the nightly news. I had already witnessed enough sadness to fill more than one lifetime. If there is a current event that I think I should know more about, I research it sufficiently to be truly knowledgeable.

I have learned not to expect affirmation from others when I tell them that I do not watch the news. In the past, the vicious verbal responses from individuals upon finding out that I quit watching the news twenty years ago would hurt my feelings. Now I let these remarks remind me that there are people who act as though keeping up with current events is a religious practice. I do not try to convert them to my way of thinking, and I try to be kind when they attempt to convert me.

Safety and Setbacks

During the first six months that I was married to Jerry, I had such extreme digestive issues that I could not function for weeks at a time. I had experienced stomachaches before, but these were much more intense. I went to a naturopath, who helped some, and yet I stayed in bed much of the time. One day, Jerry, knowing that I would feel better if I left the house, spent almost an hour gently persuading me to go to the movie *The King's Speech* with him. His attentiveness and my knowledge of self-care eventually alleviated this set back, which I understood only in retrospect. At a survivor seminar, a physician spoke about how many of his patients suffer from unusually harsh symptoms when they, for the first time in their life, experience total safety. During my newlywed days, my body was finally given an opportunity to process its past trauma.

Healing as a Job

Healing is work, and the check really is in the mail! I had a breakthrough when I learned to consider my healing efforts as my part-time job. When I was in a lot of pain and became discouraged about not accomplishing more, I started a practice each night of listing how I had spent my day. I would give special focus to time invested in recovery-related activities. This drastically changed my expectations for myself. I was happier when I finally realized that my body is my friend. If my body tells me I should slow down and relax more, I listen. I did not get a paycheck right away for my work on my own healing, but my good health is more valuable to me than any financial reward could ever be.

Dreams

Dream about a happy, healthy, productive future. I did, and my dreams came true!

My Life Now

Creative Endeavors

I feel like a huge weight has been lifted from my shoulders. My two major creative endeavors, my last feature-length documentary and my memoir, are near completion. When I dreamed about my future self—basking in the completion of these two major projects—I mostly saw myself in bed sleeping. On the days that I was especially ambitious, I thought that I would wake up for a while and read novels. I shocked myself by deciding upon a much different path. I took a weekend off to relax and to ponder my upcoming life. At age sixty-seven, I felt like a high school senior envisioning my future options. I decided to return to social work, my previous career. The idea came to me suddenly. I thought that it might go away, but it has not. I had let my social work license expire in 2010, when I started making films full time. I renewed it.

Play Therapy

My favorite role as a social worker was that of a psychotherapist for children. I have the highest credential for a social worker in my home state. It enables me to work as a counselor in private practice and receive third-party (insurance) payments. I am a trained play therapist. The Center for Play Therapy, recognized as the largest play therapy training program in the world, is on the University of North Texas's campus. In 1998, I was accepted into its exclusive two-week summer intensive program. When I attended, it was taught by founder/director Dr. Garry Landreth. There were participants from all over the world, including a school counselor from Singapore. I use the approach promoted in this training. It is called non-directive play therapy. Psychologist Dr. Carl Rogers developed non-directive therapy for adults. His approach was to simply listen to his clients. Rogers found that many people work out their own problems when they are supported by compassionate attention. I see mindful listening as my primary role as a play therapist. Play is the main way children express themselves. When a child builds a large tower, a psychoanalytic play therapist might refer to it in case notes as a phallic symbol representing unresolved deep issues. When the same thing happens in a non-directive session, the therapist says, "Tell me about what you made." This therapeutic approach recognizes children as people, not as miniature adults. It acknowledges that youngsters are capable of deep pain and joy.

I have decided to do play therapy part time, a maximum of two days a week. I want to share an office. I know one local child therapist. I met her because she was the only counselor with an available appointment when the child who was in foster care with us last December needed therapy. I was impressed with her professionalism, and with her understanding of children. When I decided to open a play therapy practice, I called her to see if I could rent her office on the weekends. She told me she now works six days, sometimes seven days, a week. There is obviously a need for another play therapist in town.

Children

With the addition of play therapy clients, my life will be filled to optimal capacity with little humans. I look forward to Wednesdays, which are my "Grandma Mary" days. Three of my grandsons live close to me. I volunteer in the cafeteria at their elementary school on a weekly basis. Along with my grandsons, both students and teachers refer to me as "Grandma Mary." One of my grandsons loves pandas, and another loves cats.

I have multiple cat dresses and panda shirts. I even found a panda dress after an extensive Internet search. I consider it an extreme honor when a grade schooler whom I do not know looks up at me and says, "I like the way you dress." I make myself useful in the lunchroom. I encourage the consumption of vegetables and remind overly talkative students to focus on eating. Sometimes I am called upon to open milk cartons, mostly by kindergarteners. As one grade level leaves the cafeteria and another enters, I help the lunchroom staff wipe off tables. When one of my grandsons is in the cafeteria with his classmates, I take a break. I sit across from him and ask about his day. I never do this for longer than two or three minutes because I know that my grandsons need time with their friends. I find that a few minutes is enough time for us to have a meaningful conversation.

I have three grandchildren—a boy and two girls—who live over 2,000 miles away. They, of course, understand why I cannot do volunteer work at their school. I will be visiting them soon, and I am delighted that my oldest granddaughter wants me to eat lunch with her at her school.

In my "Family" essay, I tell about the two little girls whom I was babysitting. I do not see one of them anymore, but the reason is a happy one. Ella's grandmother moved to town and always is available to care for her. The other little girl, Gaebe, still comes to my house weekly.

I am willing to babysit at her house, which is just a block away, but she likes my house better. She has a routine for the two or three hours she spends with me. From the moment you enter through the front door, it is obvious that my house is child friendly. The kitchenette area contains a white, child-sized table, two little pink chairs, and a miniature brown stool. When Gaebe arrives, she sits down on a pink chair, talking nonstop while I serve her a bowl of Cheerios. I sit across from her while she eats, my legs barely fitting below the white table. If she wants to make bread, we do that next so that it will have time to rise. Unless it is raining hard, Gaebe takes advantage of the fact that she is allowed to open the sliding glass door and use her imagination to play active, solitary games in our large, fenced backyard. When she comes back inside, we usually read books. Our favorite one is *Dr. De Soto*, which is about a mouse who is a dentist. Before she leaves, Gaebe plays with the stuffed animals who permanently reside in the living room on a big, comfy chair. The animals are twin pigs, adorned only with bows, and three well-clad white teddy bears in preemie baby clothes. When Gaebe decides a teddy bear requires a wardrobe change, she scrambles toward the miniature stool in the kitchen area. Under its padded seat is a storage area containing multiple ensembles suitable for fashionable teddies. Gaebe has been known to protest when her parents arrive to pick her up.

Gaebe in my backyard

My husband Jerry and I continue to be respite foster parents. Children stay with us when their full-time foster parents want (or need) a break. Foster parents are allowed two nights off per month. Normally, children stay with us for no longer than a weekend.

I call the children who come to us monthly our "regulars." When I wrote my essay "Family," we had four regulars. I am not permitted to identify children who are in foster care by name, but Kaden is no longer in care. He was reunited with his biological mother. They live in Idaho. At age thirteen, Kaden still wants to have summer visits with us, and we send him a plane ticket. My favorite part of Kaden's two-week stay this year was a ferry ride to the San Juan Islands. Instead of missing my biological grandchildren, I delighted in acting as Kaden's grandmother.

The goal of foster care is to reunite the children in care with their biological parents. When this is not possible, the homes of other relatives are considered. One of our regulars, a studious eleven-year-old whom I will call O, is currently living with us full time. He will move to another state to live with his older sister but will remain with us until the required paperwork is completed. Like Kaden, O wants to visit us every summer. Kaden and O know each other, but both have asked to come separately. Each of them want our undivided attention.

Uncertainty and loss are a part of foster care, for the foster parents as well as for the children in care. We do not see two of our "regulars" at all anymore. G is a bright child who, at age nine, asked questions like, "Who made God?" and "Why did WWI start?" He exited the foster care system to be raised by his biological grandparents. I hear that G is thriving, and I am happy for him and his relatives. At age six, D was the youngest child to come to our home for respite care. He was adorable, personable, and such a good athlete that he could outrun children who were much older than him. D's foster home was close to where we live, but that placement was disrupted, and no local home could be found for him. He was moved out of the area, and we lost track of him. I miss D.

Health

After many years of suffering from chronic pain, I now enjoy better health than most people my age do. Each week, no matter how busy I am, I do yoga multiple times, and I walk ten to twenty miles. Now that I am no longer so busy, I plan to rejoin the senior center hiking group for day-long excursions a couple of times each month.

Having fun is an important part of my ongoing healing. I can tell that I am starting to relax when I focus on cooking and baking. Last night, I looked up the recipe for French bread, which I have never made. Today I plan to put on some music and dance by myself in my bedroom.

Marriage

My husband Jerry is a great technical writer. He has edited my other essays and will edit this one as soon as I finish writing it. Jerry is also an extremely private person. I want to express my appreciation to him in this essay, but I know the best way to do that is to keep the part about him as short as possible. I will say only one thing: To Jerry's credit, he has read everything that I have written about him and has not insisted that I delete any of it.

Relatives

I am completely at peace about my lack of contact with my family of origin. My siblings have made it clear that they do not want to interact with me, and our parents are dead. I am no longer grieving the loss of these relatives. When I do think of my siblings, in my mind I wish them well. I occasionally remember heartwarming moments that I spent with one of my brothers, my younger sister, or even my mother or father. I can stay present and just be in this memory without anger or sadness. Recently I thought about the time that I made dresses for me and my sister out of yellow flowered sheets in ankle-length, Scarlett O'Hara style. My sister is fifteen years younger than me, and she took me to her kindergarten class for show-and-tell. The teacher let my sister share first, allowing me to go home without having to stay through the other presentations. I smile when I think of my sister's asking me to twirl so that we could demonstrate the fullness of our skirts.

My daughter Marly

I am thankful my sons are a part of my life. I love them. I am proud of their professional accomplishments. They are busy, and yet, they are devoted fathers. As is common among mothers of adult sons, my complaint is that they do not call me (or return my calls) as often as I would like. This does not bother me as much as it used to now that I have someone who is essentially a daughter to me. At age thirty, Marly is a few years younger than my sons. We met a year ago when she emailed me to ask questions about my film. I meet many film viewers this way, but Marly is the only one with whom I have developed a familial relationship. Like me, she is a survivor of childhood sex trafficking. She chooses to have no contact with her biological mother. Since I do not have a daughter and Marly no longer has a mother, we have adopted each other. Our relationship is just like any other healthy mother/adult daughter relationship. We confide in each other, celebrating victories and holding space for heartaches. I call Marly on the days she does not work, usually while I am on a long walk. On average, we chat at least one to two hours per week. We live across the country from each other and have only met in person once. When we were together, we talked nonstop. Our husbands also got along well. They were often asked to take photos of the two of us. I showed Marly my wedding ring and told her that she would be inheriting it, which surprised her and made her feel loved.

In case you were wondering, I will not be "adopting" anyone else.

Contact with Readers and Film Viewers

I welcome emails from readers and film viewers. To keep my body healthy and happy, I limit the time that I spend at a computer. Therefore, my replies to emails are brief. I am glad to talk on the phone to survivors and professionals who work with survivors. I currently do not charge for one-time phone calls. If I do start charging, I will offer sliding-scale fees to make them affordable for everyone. I have thought about offering life coach services to child abuse survivors via Zoom. Current information about the services that I provide always will be available on my website at:

www.MaryKnightProductions.com

Ruby's Heaven

*A fictional story inspired by my angel
connection with my mother.*

Trigger Warning: Low

Ruby pressed the back of her pearl earring into place and
admired her reflection in the entryway mirror. The rain
was falling sideways, and there was no doubt in her mind
that traffic would make her late for work, but she had to be
sure she looked perfect. Ruby always had to be sure that she
looked just perfect. If it wasn't for the glare of light that
bounced in that moment off of Ruby's hairline, she may
never have noticed. If it wasn't for that glare of light, in
fact, things may have gone quite differently that day.

What caught Ruby's attention and made her lungs
contract was not a shimmering silver or an opalescent
white, but a streak of plain gray growing from her roots
toward her chestnut strands. Ruby's hair was reflecting her
sixty-plus years of life, and if there was one thing Ruby
was resolutely against, it was looking like she'd lived sixty-plus years.

Clients could wait. Everyone could wait. Gray hair was a deal breaker.

Ruby grabbed her cell phone from her purse with shaking fingers and tapped Tess's name. In two rings she answered.

"What's up, Mom?"

Ruby couldn't control the desperation in her voice. She sounded like she was being crushed by an overturned four-wheeler.

"It's an emergency! Get to my house as quick as you can."

She could hear Tess suck in her breath, but Ruby didn't even wait for a response. Tess always came when she needed her.

***

Tess was like the piece of vintage jewelry you find at the bottom of your grandmother's top dresser drawer. Hers was the kind of beauty rare and unexpected, forgotten about for long stretches of time, and in serious need of some polishing. As Tess frantically opened her mother's front door and dropped her car keys to the ground, Ruby noticed reluctantly that her daughter was more lovely than Ruby had ever been. Her pale green eyes were arresting and her golden blond tendrils thick and shiny, even when she tangled them inside of a messy bun, piled atop her head.

"Oh thank God!" Ruby sighed from her position at the dining room table, where she was waiting with a towel, a hair dryer, and three boxes of hair dye.

Tess looked momentarily relieved before her pale gaze darkened. "This is why you called me over? This was the emergency?"

"I have gray hair, Tess, a whole wide strand of it trying

218

to take over my head. This is absolutely an emergency! I refuse to be seen like this!"

Tess closed her eyes and exhaled through her mouth. "Mom, this is ridiculous. I drove over here because I thought you'd fallen down the stairs."

Ruby knew Tess was almost past her limit, but she couldn't help herself. "Don't be dramatic, Tess."

"Dramatic? Are you kidding me? This is making me late for work. I'm not staying." Tess grabbed her keys off the floor.

Ruby softened her tone and tilted her head to one side. "I'm sorry darling, I don't want to make you late. I know that boss of yours can be terribly mean."

Tess loosened her grip on her keys. Ruby stood up and walked over to gently put her hand on her daughter's shoulder.

"You work too much, sweetheart. How many hours did you put in last week?"

"Fifty-two."

"That's absurd Tess! You practically run that place for him, and he barely pays you."

Tess's words came out tired and sad. "I know."

"I just can't stand for it!" Ruby shook her head and clucked her tongue.

"Thank you for saying that, Mom, but there's really nothing you can do."

"Why don't you call in sick today? I'll pay you to do my hair instead."

Tess brushed Ruby's hand off of her shoulder and stiffened. "It's always to get what you want, isn't it?"

Sometimes Ruby's desire to be right was stronger than her desire to be kind. "I'm not like you, Tess. I care about how I present myself to the world. You wouldn't understand. You've never been pretty."

"Why do you say stuff like that to me? You can be so mean, you know that?"

"My life was better before I had you," Ruby spat each word into the air, and each word had the sharp edge of a knife, slicing.

Without saying a word, Tess turned on her heels and threw the door back open. Ruby's last attempt at persuasion was muffled by the slam of thick mahogany wood.

"But I'm not good at doing things by myself!"

Ruby pretended like she hadn't seen Tess's lower lip quiver. She pretended like she didn't feel the impact of her words when they slapped her daughter in the heart. Ruby was good at pretending. It was how she got things done. Feeling too much slowed you down. Ruby knew this.

***

It didn't happen the way Ruby always imagined that it would. She'd envisioned a more noteworthy death—perhaps a valiant battle with cancer and last words uttered from her hospital bed as her friends and family gathered close. She'd never foreseen anything so quick or so happenstance. She was simply standing in front of the mirror, admiring her new hair color. When she lifted the hair dryer, it slipped from her hands into the sink of soapy water. Without much thought, Ruby dipped her fingers in the water to retrieve it and then everything was lightning and fire for a brief, searing instance. And then everything was light.

***

It was like flying and falling simultaneously. Whether Ruby was tumbling or leaping, she couldn't tell. But as gravity pulled in all directions, as she moved across a vast sea of shimmering gold, she could feel her body become weightless. She could feel everything changing. And then she landed.

The meadow was peppered with bluebells and lupine - sparks of indigo and carnelian amidst rolling emerald hills. It was the most fragrant, idyllic place Ruby had ever set eyes on. She tilted her head back in the warm wash of sun. That's when she noticed - someone was waiting for her.

Two tall beings with glowing faces and feathered wings stood smiling and reaching out their arms for Ruby. One was female and one was male. They wore simple clothes. The female angel spoke first, wisps of jet-black curls framing her oblong face.

"Welcome to your heaven Ruby. We are your guardians here."

Ruby's ribs suddenly felt sharp against her skin. Her stomach lurched. "Heaven? Am I dead?"

The angels nodded and continued to shower Ruby with their light-filled gaze. When Ruby searched her mind for a memory of what happened, it was blank. All she could remember was the falling and leaping sensation, the golden, shimmering sky.

"You dropped a hair dryer in a sink full of water," the male angel said gently.

"What?!"

A giggle erupted from a nearby tree and Ruby whipped her head toward the sound. A little boy with brown eyes and overalls stood watching her gleefully. The boy stepped toward her and grinned.

"I'm Andrew. I like to watch people change."

"Change? What are you talking about?" Ruby asked.

Ruby's clothes began to shrink on her body. Her bones felt squishy and then firm. Her skin felt stretched and then luminous. Ruby rubbed her forehead with her palm. Her hand felt tiny. When Ruby looked down, she found herself in a pair of black Mary Janes, white knee socks, and a blue taffeta dress. Just the kind of outfit she would have coveted when she was seven years old. She was as young as she felt.

"Do I look pretty?" she asked the boy, and the boy nodded.

"Yeah, sure. But it doesn't really matter."

"Sure it does," Ruby gasped. "It matters a lot."

"What really matters," Andrew explained, "is how you look on the inside. Isn't that right, Miss Cynthia!"

Miss Cynthia, the female guardian angel, knelt and looked straight into Ruby's eyes. "Being kind is how you grow the beauty you were born with."

At the sound of harp music, smiling children of all shapes, sizes, and ethnicities came bounding into the field from every direction.

"You got here just in time to eat," Andrew told Ruby.

A tray appeared on the lap of each youngster, and on it was their best-loved food. There were pancakes and hot dogs and steak. Milkshakes and French fries and spaghetti. At the sight of a roast beef sandwich cut in triangles and a strawberry cupcake with chocolate frosting, Ruby exclaimed, "That's my favorite!"

"We all get our favorite here. Every day," Andrew said.

As the children finished eating, Cynthia called out in a sing-song voice, "It's time to go to school." The young ones rushed to a corner of the field, and the tall male guardian angel skipped along beside them. They sat down on the ground in a circle.

Ruby and Andrew were the only stragglers. Miss Cynthia walked beside them. Ruby whined, "Do I have to go to school?"

"No, you don't. Here you decide whether to play or go to school," Miss Cynthia replied.

Pleased but confused, Ruby asked, "But don't I need to learn stuff?"

"All we need to learn is how to treat others," Andrew said. He liked teaching Ruby about heaven. "And we can learn that by playing together! Let's have a race."

Ruby was intent on ignoring Andrew. She looked around for something to do by herself and found a jump rope on the ground. Delighted, she showed off her skills, but Andrew didn't notice. With a slightly dropped chin, he turned around and scampered off in the other direction.

Miss Cynthia called out, "Andrew, don't you wander off again where you aren't allowed to go."

Ruby perked up when she found out there were rules to be broken. Jump rope still in hand, she ran after Andrew.

"Where are we not supposed to go?"

"I'll show you," Andrew said, a smile sneaking back onto his face.

After running a long way, they eventually slowed down to a gentle walk. Andrew stopped abruptly when they came upon a sign that read "No little angels beyond this point."

Ruby grabbed his hand and tried to pull him forward.

Without budging an inch, Andrew pointed to a tall wooden fence in the distance. "See that fence? It's adult heaven."

"Let's go!"

"No. We can't do that. We don't want to get hurt."

Ruby put her hands on her hips and stomped her foot. "That's just one of their stupid rules."

"It's not," Andrew argued. "Miss Cynthia explained it to me. We are in kid heaven so we can grow up. If we go to adult heaven before we're ready, it will hurt us real bad."

As Ruby ran off, she called back to him, "I don't believe that!"

With an unusual burst of speed, Andrew caught up with Ruby and tackled her. Solemnly he said, "You see things there that are too sad for kids."

"Okay," Ruby submitted. "We'll go back then."

Ruby helped Andrew up and took a few steps toward kid heaven. She let Andrew get a way in front of her, then she changed direction and sped right toward adult heaven.

Ruby surveyed the fence. It was high. Too high. Her jump rope! Swinging the rope like a lasso, Ruby secured it on the other side of the fence, where she pulled it through and tied a knot. Then she latched on like a tiny monkey and climbed to the other side.

***

Tess's day moved at the pace of a snail. It was not unusual for the hours at Cafe Henderson to drag on, especially with her boss, Cory, hovering over her shoulder and criticizing her every move. When Tess finally made her escape, an hour after close, she rushed back to her mother's house, regret gripping her belly. She hated to fight with her mother, even when her mother was cruel.

It's strange how you sense things. How the body can

feel impending danger like an animal understands the invisible warning signals of storms. It was like that for Tess, as her hand twisted around the knob. She knew, with every cell of her being, that inside she would find something awful.

"Mom?" Tess called as she moved swiftly from the entryway into the hall and toward the bathroom.

The image of her mother's body on the floor beside the sink seemed almost cartoonish at first. It was too surreal to be acceptable. It was too preventable. Tess dropped to her knees and yanked her phone from her pocket.

"911, what's your emergency?"

Tess couldn't hear herself speak, though she knew she was speaking—delivering information to the dispatcher, giving him her mother's address. All she could see was the morning replaying over and over in her mind.

"This is all your fault," a sharp voice split through her thoughts. The voice was her mother's, but it wasn't coming from her mother's body. It was as crisp and real as a slap in the face. Tess was so startled she dropped the phone.

"Someone is on their way now, ma'am," the dispatcher concluded as Tess picked the phone back up with shaking fingers.

"You heard me," the voice continued. "This is all your fault. I'm dead because of you."

The voice was coming from everywhere and nowhere, echoing inside her head until it made Tess dizzy. She folded herself into a fetal position beside her mother's body and cried like she hadn't cried since she was a baby.

***

Ruby, perched on a fence post, looked down into adult heaven. She saw a large glistening pond surrounded by a lush forest. Ruby whispered to herself, "I bet I can see my reflection in that water." She smoothed her hair and used the rope to climb down the fence. She headed toward the pond.

At the water's edge was a petite woman with a long braid and smooth brown skin. Brown moccasins adorned her tiny feet and long yellow feathers hung from her ears. A new woman took form beside her. She had a thoughtful expression, but all Ruby noticed was her large stomach, her too-tight dress, and her purplish lipstick.

"Welcome to heaven, Miss Thompson. My name is Violet," the petite woman said. "You had a heart attack while you were teaching."

Miss Thompson's face contorted in surprise. "Oh, no! My first graders had to see that. Are they okay?"

Violet nodded. "The principal is with them."

Miss Thompson sighed in relief. "I don't mean to seem ungrateful, but I never wanted to go to heaven. I wanted to teach forever."

"Oh, you can do that here. But first, you get a chance to see how your life affected the people you loved. Do you ever wonder about your students? The ones you lost touch with?"

Miss Thompson's eyes grew wide. "Of course."

The petite angel inquired, "Which ones?"

"All of them. But especially the ones who already had a hard life."

"Like Bobby Bell?"

Miss Thompson's eyes showed her concern, "Oh, Bobby. I was just furious when he had to move during the middle of the year to go to his fourth foster home."

Violet motioned toward the lake. The frumpy teacher looked into it and saw her reflection only for a moment. Then she saw six-year-old Bobby Bell. His chubby face changed into the face of Dr. Robert Bell. Dr. Bell was in an

African village examining a child who looked a lot like he did when he was young.

"You convinced Bobby he was smart enough to learn to read. He never experienced love until he met you."

Miss Thompson, overcome with emotion, turned to the angel, and hugged her.

While no one was looking her way, Ruby ran toward the water. She stared into the pond and saw the reflection of her disheveled image for a split second. Then she saw a young woman crying on the floor beside the body of a dead old lady.

And even though the dead old lady didn't speak, an older voice resounded in the room as the younger woman cried. The voice was sharp and relentless.

"You killed me!" it echoed. "It's all your fault!"

"Who is saying those mean words?" Ruby asked, wide-eyed.

As soon as Ruby spoke, the angel and the teacher noticed her. Violet said, "Miss Thompson, this never happens."

In the consoling tone adults who are not adept with children use when talking to them, Violet said, "I need to take you back to kid heaven. Something fun is going on there."

Ruby wanted to ignore the loud, vindictive words but just couldn't. She hung her head.

In an overly cheerful voice, Violet said, "Your favorite dessert is waiting for you in kid heaven! Let's go."

Ruby looked down again. This time she recognized her daughter. "That's Tess. She's my daughter."

Violet tried hard to distract Ruby. "How could you have a daughter? You're just a little girl."

Ruby's lip quivered. "I don't know how she can be my daughter, but I know she is. And that mean old bag is me!"

Miss Thompson couldn't stand it any longer. She might not be an angel, but she knew what children needed. "This is a travesty. Look how heartbroken she is!" Miss Thompson plopped onto the ground, offering Ruby her lap. Ruby crumbled into Miss Thompson's lap and hung onto her.

In a strict schoolteacher tone, Miss Thompson demanded, "You've got to tell her the truth. Right now!"

Even angels obey angry teachers. "That was indeed you," Violet informed Ruby. "You simply changed when you got to heaven. You see, here in heaven, you reflect the age you were on the inside when you were alive."

The voice and the young woman's sobs grew louder.

"Why does she hear those mean words if I'm dead?"

"She got so used to listening to them when you were alive that she can't figure out how to stop it," Violet explained.

"I want to go back. I want to go back and help her." Ruby pleaded.

"When you grow up, you can go down and talk to her if you want, but not yet."

"But it will take me years to grow up. That's not fair!"

"You can grow up really fast in heaven, Ruby," Violet said truthfully. "The more you learn, the faster you grow."

"Please, please!" Ruby stood up and pointed toward the water. "I need to go help her right now!"

Ruby became inconsolable. She cried out in agony. Her despair seemed endless.

Miss Thompson was outraged, "Who is in charge here? This child needs real help."

That's when a new figure appeared—distant at first, like a luminous sphere. As the sphere drew closer, Ruby realized it was someone she had always known but never seen. A pure beauty with dark skin, blue eyes, and black cotton-candy hair. Her smile enchanted Ruby. As she got closer, she took the shape of a kind-looking man in faded jeans. He sat down beside Miss Thompson and placed his hand on Ruby's tiny shoulder. He looked at Ruby with a gaze that felt like a soft song or a welcome embrace or a perfect rain.

The angel stood as tall as she could possibly stand and said, "God, I wish I'd handled this better."

The old man addressed the angel calmly. As he did, his skin tone changed to match hers.

"We'll set you up with some additional training. Miss Thompson is right. Ruby knows too much. She can't be happy here until this is resolved."

God's skin tone darkened as he nodded a thank-you to Miss Thompson.

Ruby looked into God's eyes, which changed to blue. He placed his now-white hand on Ruby's head. He let out a long, low whistle and the golden shimmer returned.

***

Tess stayed back after the men took her mother's body. She returned to her spot on the floor where her mother once laid. She didn't feel the presence of the small child standing behind her, but she heard the child's soft exhale.

Her first thought was that grief had made her crazy.

"That woman was so mean to you. You shouldn't listen to her."

Tess rubbed her eyes and blinked. The small child still stood before her, with shiny black shoes and rosy cheeks.

"Excuse me?"

The voice returned, this time louder than before. It echoed around Tess and the child. "You're wasting your life at that job! What's wrong with you? You'll never do anything great."

The child recoiled and put her chubby hands on her hips. "That's mean! You leave her alone!"

"You can hear that too?" Tess asked as a single tear rolled down her cheek.

"Of course I can. She talks so loud!"

"Am I the only one who can see you?"

"Don't know," the little girl replied.

***

Even the worst boss gives you time off when your mother dies. During her three days of personal leave, Tess saw the small child only once.

Tess, alone in her room, held up three dresses. She simply couldn't decide which one to wear to her mother's funeral.

The little girl materialized and, without comment, grabbed two of the dresses and hung them back in the closet.

Tess went back to work the day after burying her mother. The small child was doing a cartwheel when Tess's boss walked right past her without blinking an eye.

"Guess you're the only one who can see me," the youngster said between cartwheels.

"There are two customers waiting for drinks. Can't you work any faster?!" Tess's boss barked as he sat down at a corner table. He was a stocky man with thinning hair and a mouth that never smiled.

"I'm getting to it right now," Tess replied meekly as her cheeks burned pink.

"Why doesn't he just help you if he wants it done so fast?" the child demanded.

"Because some people don't believe in helping others. They only want to help themselves."

The child felt something stirring inside her chest when Tess spoke. A memory that had no pictures but felt like regret. She looked down at the counter and frowned. Tess placed a warm palm on the child's back. Her voice was soft as a blanket.

"It's okay, honey. It's a waste of time to worry about what other people do. It's more important to make sure you're being the best you that you can be."

The child perked up. "You should have more fun. Let's go play." Ruby did a tap dance ending with a bow.

"I can't," Tess giggled. "I'm still at work." She hesitated and then smiled. "But when I'm off, it's a date."

***

Grief came in waves, like a changing sea. One moment Tess could breathe and the next she felt like a fish out of water.

But the presence of that little being, even if it made her question her sanity, soothed something in Tess. It felt comforting, like home.

After work, she took the young one to a carnival because, when she was a kid, Tess loved carnivals. The child's eyes were bright with glee as they wandered around the grounds, gazing at the big lit-up Ferris wheel making its slow turn through the sky.

"Want to eat something?" the child asked. She grabbed Tess's hand to pull her toward a stand with pictures of corn dogs and juicy burgers.

"What do you want, little one?" Tess whispered, as they approached an apron-clad man with a fat mustache.

"How about a hot dog?"

"Okay."

"And a hamburger!"

"Sounds good," Tess smiled.

"And curly fries!" the child exclaimed. Tess couldn't contain her laughter.

"This guy's going to think I'm extra hungry, but here goes," she whispered.

At a picnic table below the Ferris wheel, the child surveyed the food and then looked at Tess with a mischievous grin.

"It's for you."

"What?"

"I don't get hungry. I'm not like you."

"I can't eat all this food." Tess shook her head. "But that was sweet of you, little one."

"I bet you can. Why don't you try?"

As Tess looked into the child's bright blue eyes, she felt like a little kid herself. Her belly rumbled, and for the first time in a long while, Tess felt free and happy and relaxed. Under the glow of the carnival lights, against the backdrop of thrilled shrieks and upbeat music, Tess ate until she wasn't hungry, and the small child chattered about small child things and the world felt like everything was in its rightful place.

***

One night soon after the carnival, the little girl and Tess were sitting in Tess's small apartment, drawing. The child noticed that Tess's pictures were better than what adults usually drew.

"You're really good at that," the child told her while she finished coloring in the pink tutu of a graceful ballerina. Tess put the final touches on a rippling ocean she'd been working on for hours.

"I'm not that great," Tess mumbled without looking up from her drawing.

"Are too," the little one shot back. Tess was silent. "You aren't very good at saying thank you," the child added. This time Tess looked up, and her eyes watered.

"You're right," she said. "I'm not used to getting compliments. I haven't had a lot of practice."

"Well, practice makes perfect," the young one said in a sing-song way. Tess reached out to squeeze her hand.

"You're pretty smart, you know that?" Tess said, and the child smiled up at her.

***

Tess was late coming home, like usual, but this time she'd left the youngster at her house and felt concerned as she pushed open the front door at half past eight. The little girl furrowed her brows and stuck out her lower lip.

"Did your boss make you stay late again?"

"Yeah, but it's okay," Tess responded cheerfully. "I'm home now."

"He's lazy. He could help you, but he doesn't."

"He's not so bad," Tess countered.

That's when the voice returned, loud and sharp, her mother's piercing cadence echoing through the house. "He is too!" the voice shouted in unison with the small child.

Tess sucked in her breath. "You agree on something," she said to the big open space where the voice had just been.

The child stood up and walked toward Tess. She wrapped her tiny fingers around Tess's hand. "I don't like the way he treats you," she said, and her eyes grew round.

The voice was quick to follow up. "He's mean, he's arrogant, and he only thinks of himself."

"Kind of like you!" the child shouted in the wake of the voice's last words. "You're mean and selfish, just like him!"

"That's ridiculous!" the voice argued. "I'm nothing like him."

The child set her fierce stare on Tess, and Tess couldn't help but nod her head. "You are," Tess said softly, and the voice grew in volume.

"Even if I was like him, there's nothing I can do about it now! It's not like it would help for me to apologize. What's done is done."

Tess took a deep breath that traveled from her toes to her heart. When she spoke, her voice was clear.

"It would help," she said. Everything, for a moment, was silent.

"I have nothing to apologize for," the voice responded. Tess could feel her throat constrict.

The child's face burned scarlet, and her little fists clenched. "You're so mean! Apologize right now!"

"Why don't you do it for me?" the voice demanded. "After all, we're the same person."

The child bit her lip and shook her head. Tess felt like all the air was leaving her body.

"That's not true," the child sighed.

"It is true," the voice continued. "You grow up to be me."

"I'm not you. I'm nice!"

"Do you want to see a picture of me at her age, Tess?" the voice asked.

Tess barely managed to utter yes. On the ground at her feet, a small photograph materialized with the simplicity of steam rising. The photo was the little girl, but in Tess's grandparents' home. Tess looked up into the child's eyes, and in that moment, she saw her mother. She saw her mother as a vulnerable kid, all the beauty that got twisted by anger still in its original state of innocence and joy. The small child locked eyes with Tess, and their mutual tears were unrestrained.

"I hurt you so much," Ruby whimpered, a fat teardrop falling from the corner of her eye down to her chin. "I'm so sorry, Tess. I'm so, so sorry."

Tess wrapped her arm around Ruby's little shoulders and pulled her close. "Shhhh, little one, it's okay."

"Why was I so mean to you?"

Tess couldn't find any words. There was only her own confusion.

"I don't know."

"God," a frustrated Ruby called out, "I have a question for you." She tilted her head toward the ceiling. Tess looked up and saw a woman of no particular ethnicity, or, perhaps, of every ethnicity, with dark skin; black curls; blue, slanted eyes; high cheek bones; and a compassionate smile. She was both muscular and beautiful in a way that made Tess aware of her own power and goodness. The woman turned around, and instead of seeing her back, Tess saw a wise old man in worn jeans with skin the same color as hers.

He knelt down in front of Ruby and looked her in the eyes as he said, "Someday, you will understand, but you're not old enough yet. Your daughter is old enough, however. If she wants to know, I can show her. You need to play while we have an adult conversation."

If someone had told Tess three weeks ago that she'd be talking to God through her living room ceiling and communicating with the child version of her deceased mother, she would have assumed she'd been checked into a mental institution. Instead, looking at the rugged but tender face, she felt the same way she did at the carnival. Like everything was in its rightful place.

Ruby pulled away from Tess's warm embrace, then marched stoically out of the room.

"I'm ready for what you have to show me," announced a trembling Tess.

The window began to shimmer and blur until Tess was looking at a different moment—one from before she came to be. Her grandfather, Adam, sat on the couch in her mother's childhood home. Her grandmother, Pearl, busied herself in the kitchen.

"When is Ruby getting here with that boyfriend of hers?" Adam said gruffly.

"When she gets here, don't make her more nervous that she already is, Adam!" Pearl hollered from the kitchen.

"She should be nervous," he spat. "I don't want my daughter dating just anybody." Adam scratched his belly, then added, "Did you get dinner ready yet?" His tone hadn't the faintest edge of gratitude.

"I'm not fond of that man either, Adam," Pearl huffed, but before she could finish her discourse, the doorbell rang. Pearl swiftly opened the door to find Ruby standing beside a young man. He was handsome, with the same pale green eyes and thick golden-blond hair as Tess.

Tess had been watching in silence, but since this was the first time she had ever seen her father, she couldn't help but blurt out, "That's my dad! We look alike." God nodded but made no comment.

Tom had one hand on his hip, as if to imply that Pearl had made them wait too long. "Mom, Dad, you remember Tom Wilson," Ruby grinned, ushering her boyfriend inside and closing the door.

Adam grunted. Pearl offered a strained smile and said, "Lovely to see you again."

"I still can't believe you're not sisters," Tom said. Pearl flinched.

"Can I talk to you in the kitchen, sweetheart?" Pearl planted a concerned gaze, and Ruby nodded her head.

"I'm going to help my mom in the kitchen, Tom. You stay out here and relax."

Tom's brow furrowed. "Don't take too long, will ya?"

In the kitchen, Pearl pulled Ruby by the wrist into the farthest corner of the room. "I'm telling you, Ruby, I don't like him. I don't like him one bit."

Ruby's cheeks blazed and her eyes watered.

"You don't even know him, Mom. You're not giving him a chance."

"I don't need to know him. I can see it a mile away. He's a smooth-talking, self-centered, immature man, and he's no good. I'm telling you, Ruby."

"If you really feel that way," Ruby said in a low voice that was firm and stubborn, "then we're not staying for dinner."

"Don't get back into that man's car."

"Don't tell me what to do."

And with that, Ruby stormed out of the kitchen and grabbed Tom by the arm. "Let's go. We're not welcome here."

They jumped into Tom's car and sped out of the

driveway and onto the graveled country road. Instead of heading toward town, Tom turned onto a dead-end dirt road and parked.

"What are we doing here?"

Tom unbuckled his seatbelt and latched his hand onto Ruby's knee. "I went all the way over to your parents' house with you for dinner, and we got kicked out. I think you owe me!"

"What are you talking about?"

"I think you owe me a better night." Tom's voice had a strange edge, his words hollow and wooden.

Ruby shook her head and brushed his hand aside, but he grabbed her wrists instead. "Don't fight me," he hissed.

That's when Tess squeezed her eyes shut and let tears race down her cheeks while the sound of her mother's screams echoed through the space.

***

A much-changed Tess sat on the sofa, exhausted and shocked. Ruby entered the room and cuddled up beside her.

"I'm so sorry that happened to you," Tess whispered. Ruby didn't understand what Tess meant, but she could feel that it was important. The voice echoed around them, but this time, all its sharpness had dissolved. It was tender and afraid.

"It wasn't that bad, really."

"Yes, it was," Tess said firmly. "Everything was different for you after that night. Your life really was better before you had me."

The voice relinquished words and instead cried softly. Ruby didn't know exactly why she said what she said next, but it made sense to her in some way she couldn't explain.

"Do you want to grow up now?" she asked the voice.

"I want to quit being mean," the voice said softly.

Ruby jumped up and yelled decisively, "God, we're ready."

Tess knelt down and looked into Ruby's eyes.

"Thank you," Tess murmured. "I'll miss you so much."

Tess put her arms around Ruby's small frame. It felt good to hug Ruby one last time! As Tess squeezed tighter, Ruby's body liquified. Tess ended up hugging herself. She stared as Ruby transformed into a tiny tornado of pale blue glitter. White glitter erupted from the corners of the room and joined the twister. The whirlwind danced up to the ceiling and vanished.

When Tess was alone, she sat for a long time in silence. She put her hand to her heart and felt her mother's pain slowly weave a new story of redemption. She envisioned the old man's kind eyes and endless warmth. Tess reflected on the radiant woman's power and loveliness, which, in turn, caused her to acknowledge her own strength and beauty. She heard little Ruby's sweet giggle and felt her protective fierceness. Tess took a deep breath and reminded herself of a truth she'd always known.

She was human. It was never too late to grow up.

***

On a bench by the river, Tess gazed at the soft dusk braiding purples and pale blues through the mist of evening. Today was a good day—her last day at the cafe. Cory hadn't expected her to quit, but she no longer cared about his expectations. A whole new world of possibilities spread out before her, and she closed her eyes. She listened to the gentle rhythm of footsteps, laughter, and conversation. In the dimming of the day she inquired, with the sweet innocence of a child, "Tess, what makes you happy?"

Epilogue

The sign was painted in big blue letters above a handsome oak door. Little Ruby's Art Café was a place for both the coffee connoisseur and the art enthusiast. It was where people came to talk, to sip dark roast, to buy art, and to stock up on supplies. Tess's brainchild—part café, part art shop, part gallery—took off quicker than she could have ever imagined. It suited her to be in charge like this. She knew how to create space for the community. She knew how to be graceful and how to be strong. In the back corner of the room, Tess sat beside her easel, admiring another painting she'd completed from her little angel series. This one showed Ruby tap dancing.

Her two employees, Doug and Laura, busied themselves with cleanup, while they sang out of tune to local radio music.

"We had a great day, Tess," Laura smiled as she closed the register and made a note in the café log.

"It's always a great day for me when I sell more than one painting." Tess grinned.

A loud clatter made Laura jump. Doug quickly emerged with flushed cheeks and an apologetic frown.

"I broke a bunch of glasses! I'm so sorry, Tess."

"Don't worry about it."

Doug nodded his head as Laura handed him a broom. Tess suddenly felt goosebumps cover her skin and the temperature shift in the air around her. When she looked to her left, her mother was standing in front of her, exactly how she was before she died, except with a mane of gorgeous gray hair.

"I came to apologize to you, my beautiful daughter."

Tess couldn't feel her own breath, just a wash of emotion and the desire to be held.

"Everyone makes mistakes," Tess said.

Doug responded from behind the counter where he swept glass into a small bin.

"Thank you for being so understanding about it, Tess."

Tess didn't turn her head toward Doug. She focused on her mother. She didn't want to miss a second of this precious moment.

Tess sank into her mother's embrace. She let her head rest on her mother's shoulder like she did when she was a little girl. She let time evaporate and the pain rise and dissolve. Tess let everything go as her mother squeezed her tight and the rules of visible and invisible ceased to matter.

In the cozy glow of evening, surrounded by her creativity and her future, Tess let her mother love her. Tess let her past be healed, with the gracious ease of light reclaiming morning.

Printed in Great Britain
by Amazon

25136453R00142